A Torch in Flame

The story of a county cricket club at war: following 5 Hampshire cricketers during the First World War

© Peter Jones 2014
ISBN 9781897887493

This edition published in 2014 by Natula Publications
and printed in the UK.

The author has asserted his rights under the Copyright, Designs and
Patent Act 1988 to be identified as the author of the work.

Acknowledgments

As someone who grew up listening to the soft burr of John Arlott, it was natural that I should start this project by reading his account of the development of the Hampshire side up to and after the catastrophe of World War 1. Hampshire CC Archivist Dave Allen was kind enough to lend me a battered copy of *Hampshire County Cricket* from 1957, co-written by Messrs Arlott, Eagar, Altham and Webber. *The History of Hampshire Cricket Club* by Peter Wynne-Thomas (Guild Publishing, 1988) was also invaluable, and features a foreword by the Cricketing Sage of Basingstoke. Sir Derek Birley's *A Social History of English Cricket* (Aurum Press, 2000) gave me a real grasp of the wider context of the game a hundred years back, and is an excellent read. Clive Harris and Julian Whippy have done a great deal of work on sportsmen whose careers were cut short by the conflict, and their book *The Greater Game: Sporting Icons who fell in the Great War* (Pen and Sword, 2008) was so well researched that I nearly gave up on the spot!

On the individual cricketers I cover here, Edwin Astill's edition of *The Great War Diaries of Brigadier-General Alexander Johnston 1914-1917* (Pen and Sword, 2007) gives the reader a superb insight into the career of a WW1 officer. The background on the Worcester Regiment soldiers who were executed comes from Julian Putkowski and Julian Sykes' *Shot at Dawn* (Leo Cooper, 2007).

The chapter on Jaques features an analysis of the ill fated Loos campaign of 1915, and for this account Niall Cherry's book, *Most Unfavourable Ground* (Helion and Company, 2008) was indispensable.

The context for Cecil Abercrombie's demise at sea was provided by Nigel Steel and Peter Hart's excellent *Jutland 1916* (Cassel 2003).

Hesketh-Pritchard's own account of his war years, *Sniping in France*, has just been reprinted by the Foreman Press.

Lionel, Lord Tennyson's autobiographical pieces (*From Verse to Worse* and *Sticky Wickets*) were entertaining: wonderful insights into the man himself as much as accounts of his war experiences. I have been asked which of these brave men I would most like to have met. His Lordship wins hands down. My interest in the period was sparked by reading Alan Edward's biography *Lionel Tennyson: Regency Buck* (Robson Books, 2001).

Last but not least. My thanks to Dave Allen, Hampshire's tireless Archivist, who has been supportive from the first time we met to discuss the idea. If you've been good enough to buy this book, you might consider treating yourself to his book *150 Not Out*, which charts 150 years of Hampshire Cricket history.

Peter Jones 2014

Contents

Vitai Lampada

(*Torch of Life*)

There's a breathless hush in the Close to-night -
Ten to make and the match to win -
A bumping pitch and a blinding light,
An hour to play and the last man in.
And it's not for the sake of a ribboned coat,
Or the selfish hope of a season's fame,
But his Captain's hand on his shoulder smote
"Play up! play up! and play the game!"

The sand of the desert is sodden red, -
Red with the wreck of a square that broke; -
The Gatling's jammed and the colonel dead,
And the regiment blind with dust and smoke.
The river of death has brimmed his banks,
And England's far, and Honour a name,
But the voice of schoolboy rallies the ranks,
"Play up! play up! and play the game!"

This is the word that year by year
While in her place the School is set
Every one of her sons must hear,
And none that hears it dare forget.
This they all with a joyful mind
Bear through life like a torch in flame,
And falling fling to the host behind -
"Play up! play up! and play the game!"

Sir Henry Newbolt, 1892

The towering urgencies of war

The Hampshire countryside, or more specifically, the River Itchen, was where Sir Edward Grey went to get away from it all. The Foreign Secretary had plenty to occupy his thoughts in the summer of 1914 as Europe headed for catastrophe. Grey used to stay in a cottage in Itchen Abbas, and he would fish and make ornithological notes. As the summer wore on, it must have been more and more difficult to find peace. On the eve of war, he is credited with the doom laden words, supposedly said to his Private Secretary – "The lamps are going out all over Europe, we shall not see them lit again in our life-time." The "Great War" would eventually account for approximately 37 million people dead and wounded. In Britain, over 3 million men would be killed or wounded.

One of Grey's metaphorical "lamps" was sport, which was inevitably due to be severely curtailed as the country was plunged into a new phenomenon – "total war". Players and spectators alike were in the throes of a moral crisis. With the country at war, should they be seen to be engaging in leisure activities? Lord Roberts, the crusty old Boer war veteran, felt that "This is not the time to play Games". Sir Arthur Conan-Doyle, the creator of Sherlock Holmes, a cricketing nut and part time goalkeeper for Portsmouth at Fratton Park declared, "If a footballer has strength of limb, let them serve and march in the field of battle." As a 55 year old, he had been turned down by the War Office when he offered his services, and clearly felt that younger, fitter men were obliged to "do their bit".

The MCC refused to buckle as this popular pressure built up in the late summer of 1914, saying that "no good purpose can be saved at the moment by cancelling matches." Perhaps they felt that cricket was performing an important task as a means of releasing some tension. Perhaps the MCC feared that they had too much to lose. Prior to the outbreak of war, County cricket was in a "Golden Age". Crowds were increasing, and the resultant revenue stream was allowing counties to pay for a new breed of cricketer, the professional. Now the cricketing powers could see high profile individuals such as Archie White, the captain of Yorkshire, and Lionel Tennyson, the new star in the Hampshire batting line up, were having to leave the County scene in order to join their units. Another star, Jack Hobbs, had to move his benefit match from the Oval because the ground had become an army camp. Finally, the MCC's attempts to promote a "business as usual" approach were torpedoed by the game's greatest name, W.G. Grace. On the 27th of August his letter was published in *The Sportsman:*

"There are many cricketers who are already doing their duty, but there are many more who do not seem to realize that in all probability they will have to serve either at home or abroad before the war is brought to a conclusion. The fighting on the Continent is very severe and will probably be prolonged. I think the time has arrived when the county cricket season should be closed, for it is not fitting at a time like this that able-bodied men should be playing cricket by day and pleasure-seekers look on. I should like to see all first-class cricketers of suitable age set a good example and come to the help of their country without delay in its hour of need."

The Good Doctor's words carried considerable weight. Soon the County Championship was suspended from 1915 to 1918, with leaders Surrey declared the winners. The ever popular Scarborough Festival was shut down as "the continuation of first-class cricket is hurtful to the feelings of a section of the public". The cricketing "lamps" were also going out across the Empire. In Australia, the Sheffield Shield was also suspended until the 1919–20 season. First-class cricket disappeared in South Africa until a series of matches against the touring Australian Imperial Forces Cricket Team in 1919. The very last County cricket match in England came to a tame, rather distracted draw at Hove. In one of the ironies of history, the same two sides, Sussex and Yorkshire, played out the very last game before the Second World War brought the curtain down on first class cricket twenty five years and a day later.

Sportsmen were seen, as Conan Doyle suggested, as the epitome of the perfect fighting man. Young, fit and courageous, their recruitment would be used by the War Office to encourage others to join. The 17th battalion of the Middlesex Regiment's recruitment posters urged men to "Play the Greater Game" over in France, and it proved to be a successful campaign, with the so called Sportsman's Battalion being heavily oversubscribed. Up in Scotland, Sir George McCrae used the Heart of Midlothian football team as a recruitment tool. "You are strong: be willing", his newspaper advertisement cried. Sixteen of the Hearts squad joined the colours, followed by droves of enthusiastic supporters. The 16th Royal Scots became known as "McCrae's Battalion", earning a reputation as a tough fighting force. Seven members of the all-conquering pre-war Hearts football side were never to hear the roar of the Tynecastle faithful again.

The Times of 6th September 1914, in an article entitled "Patriotism Before Sport" describes how "Eight Hampshire County cricket professionals – Mead, Newman, Kennedy, Remnant, Livsey, Evans, Boyes, and Dibden – have enlisted in a body in the 5th Hants Territorials." This unit formed part of the Wessex battalion, and was stationed initially at Carlton Place in Southampton. Soon they were transferred to Bulford for training before being shipped to India. They landed in Karachi on 11th November 1914, and Hampshire cricket fans would not see this talented group of players at the County Ground for nearly five long years.

Alec Johnston

Alec Johnston (left) and A.K. Campbell (right)

Alexander Johnston was a career soldier who fought from the summer of 1914 to the autumn of 1917, when he was seriously wounded and returned home. Born into an army family in Derby in 1884, he was the son of Col. Sir Duncan Johnston KCMG, CB, CBE. who also played first class cricket as an opening batsman for Derbyshire. Alexander went to Winchester College, where he was an outstanding sportsman, and left school to finish his education at RMC Sandhurst. By 1903, he was a 2nd Lieutenant in the Worcester Regiment, and a full Lieutenant in 1907. He had made his first class debut at the County Ground, Southampton in July 1902 against Surrey, and played as regularly as his army commitments allowed. A posting to Nigeria between 1907 and 1910 with the West Africa Frontier Force gave him the opportunity to widen his horizons, as well as to earn hockey and polo caps for his adopted home country. There are several international sportsmen on the Hampshire books, but not too many can lay claim to such an exotic sporting c.v. Johnston also spent some time living the life of a cowboy in New Mexico and Colorado.

Johnston played cricket for Hampshire on his return. 1912 proved to be his golden summer, described by H.S. Altham as the year Johnston "reached his full maturity as a batsman." The highlight, said Altham, was a "truly wonderful innings of 89 against Sydney Barnes at his best on a horribly lively wicket" for the Gentlemen at Lord's. For Hampshire, he was part of a then record second wicket stand of 250 runs with the legendary Phillip Mead at Coventry against Warwickshire, a match where he also achieved the rare feat of scoring a century in each innings. That summer he missed playing for an MCC team against the touring Australians because he could not be contacted in time for the start of the match, which is in itself an insight into the prevailing amateur ethos of the game at that time! Over his Hampshire career, he scored over 5000 runs at a decent average of 30.74. The match at Coventry gave him his highest ever score of 175, and he managed to score ten centuries during his first class career. One wonders what he might have achieved in the game if his professional calling had not rendered him unavailable so regularly. It is interesting to note that his army commitments badly affected the 1913 season, and his form dropped away.

When war was declared after the hot summer of 1914 Johnston had been promoted to the post of Signals Officer for the 7th Infantry Brigade. They were ordered to mobilise at Tidworth on the afternoon of 4th August. On the morning of the 13th of August they left the camp and arrived at Southampton docks that afternoon, but a delay meant that they did not sail for France until the following evening.

For all our twenty-first century cynicism towards the British railway system, it is fascinating to note that the massive task of transporting all the troops of the British Expeditionary Force from their barracks and training camps to the ships was an impressive logistical success. Like

Johnston's Worcester Regiment, most arrived at Southampton early, some having to spend a night camping out on Southampton Common before their boats were ready for embarkation. When the Worcesters were finally aboard, the men endured a miserable crossing in rough seas and pouring rain. It must have been a sobering experience for the soldiers who had left Tidworth in such an enthusiastic frame of mind. It was all the more sobering for their quartermaster who fell overboard during disembarkation at Rouen.

The First World War is popularly characterised by its lack of movement, a conflict dominated by images of trenches, barbed wire and machine guns. In the early weeks of 1914 however the BEF was pitched into a war of rapid movement, on similar terms, and indeed similar territory, to the epic struggles fought in this part of Europe at the start of the nineteenth century. What the historian Richard Holmes called the "fatal avenue" of Flanders and Picardy was once again the setting for a war of initially fluid tactical manoeuvring as each side attempted to outflank their opponent. The BEF, famously described as "the contemptible little army" by the Kaiser, had to respond quickly to the German thrust through Belgium and Northern France towards Paris.

The Worcesters left Rouen, marching through Marbaix, Avesnes and Feignies. They were heading to the Belgian town of Mons, and as Johnston marched his men along the pavé in Flanders he had no reason to believe this campaign would be any different to those fought against Napoleon, conflicts that he had discussed and studied during his time at Sandhurst. The next four years were to change military thinking forever.

Johnston's Diaries at this stage are full of acute observations on the detail of the French defensive positions he passed as the Worcesters marched eastwards – indeed, throughout his Diaries, he shows himself to have been a deep thinker on trench warfare. It is interesting to see that even at this early stage in the war, with his nineteenth century preconceptions as yet unrattled by machine guns, he is quick to take note of the French "digging in" on the frontier. In an early indicator of the establishment of a line of trenches from the Swiss border to the English Channel, he correctly spotted that the French were already considering the advantages of holding a strong position. The Worcesters, in the vanguard of the BEF, pushed on into Belgium.

On August 24th Johnston and his men made contact with the Kaiser's forces at the town of Mons. He proved himself to be an energetic leader of men, bravely risking his life to move from one unit to the next to establish clear instructions across the line. It was soon obvious that their position was hopeless.

The numerical superiority of the German forces threatened to overwhelm the BEF, and an orderly retreat had to be executed. "One got a slight idea of what a terrible thing defeat in war may be," he writes. After failing to save "Brave little Belgium", the men of the BEF were faced with the prospect of going back the way they had come, a thoroughly depressing prospect for Johnston. He was aware of the need for his men to see him conducting this operation calmly and with strength of purpose. He noted that as he organised a rearguard action on the outskirts of the village of Caudry, troops from other units were flooding back in some disorder. "It makes me sad and anxious for the future to see Englishmen behave like this..." These were professional troops, of course, some of them Boer War veterans, and Johnston would have expected these men to be disciplined and steady under fire. Later on in the war, as we shall see, he had to come to terms with dealing with raw recruits and conscripts. He set his standards high although history should note that he was not doing so from some remote chateau. Indeed, as the Germans fought his men at Caudry, Johnston realised that a part of the defensive line outside the village was exposed, and he led a group of men out beyond the defensive ring to plug the gap. They crawled out into a turnip field, where they were able to bat off a German attack. The enemy artillery responded, however, and Johnston suffered a shrapnel wound to the thigh. Another piece of shrapnel punched a hole in his chest pocket, where it came to rest, and he fished it out at the Advanced Dressing Station back in the village a few hours later.

After treatment, he rejoined the unit as it left Caudry. The line of their retreat took them along the modern day D932, heading westwards, with the accurate German artillery keeping them moving from one battered village to the next. He describes the town of Estrees as a "wretched sight...broken down carts, discarded equipment, dead horses, meat and other food lying by the roadside, and stragglers of most regiments on all sides..."

Four years on, a young Manchester Regiment officer would win an MC for his bravery down the road from Estrees at Joncourt. Wilfred Owen and his men would be heading eastwards and the discarded equipment would all be German.

Johnston and his men covered 125 miles in 5 days. They had marched through the night on two occasions, had been allowed little or no sleep, and had fought a series of battles along the way. Now, in relative safety after they crossed the Aisne river, they had what Johnston described as their first day's rest since they left Tidworth. Johnston himself lay down on some cobblestones in the village of Sancy and slept.

Inevitably, the Germans were tired too. They had the extra logistical problem of keeping themselves supplied, and had to fight against troops who had managed to slow them down with some clever and very brave rearguard actions. All this held them up, and the very essence of the Germans' Schlieffen Plan was that the thrust towards Paris was to be swift if it was to be decisive. The Kaiser and his High Command were already looking nervously over their shoulders as the Tsar's massive army formed up at the starting gate. The Retreat from Mons may have been a depressing experience for the BEF, but the controlled nature of its execution had a profound effect on the outcome of the war. The war could well have been over by Christmas, but not in the way envisaged by the newspapers back in England.

With trench lines being dug, the early war of movement and night marches was over, and the Worcesters were transferred to Flanders.

15

Johnston won an MC for his leadership in the teeth of a succession of German attacks near Neuve Chapelle, again showing a clear sense that he believed that a strong leader needed to be in the front line. He rarely wavered from this belief throughout the war, despite his promotion to the higher echelons, and his immediate superiors would have to order him to stay away from the frontline trenches on several occasions.

Depressingly, Christmas of 1914 found the troops in well-established trenches, and recent engagements suggested that they were in for the long haul. Johnston spent the day with a group of fellow officers in the smoke filled remains of a house in Kemmel, where some attempt had been made to create a turkey dinner. Johnston continued to place an important emphasis on the home comforts in maintaining morale. He quickly appreciated that the troops who were able to deal with the appalling conditions of the winter trenches were going to be better fighters. His unit countered the wet trenches by standing sentries in upright open wooden barrels, where they could at least keep their feet dry. His diaries continue to log his movements, showing again that he was an energetic, concerned leader of his troops.

Despite his promotion to the Staff of 3rd Division early in 1915, Johnston still found himself out of step with the conduct of the war. He was at once critical of their outmoded methods, particularly with respect to their deployment and use of artillery, but also deeply unhappy with the Allied use of the latest technology - poison gas. Quite simply, he felt that his side was guilty of not "playing the game". He was angry by what he saw as the Allies following the German lead. He notes the high levels of arsenic in the water supply, and assumes (probably correctly) that the enemy was poisoning the water supply. The Ypres salient was so important strategically that all manner of weapons were trialled in the sector, including the introduction of liquid fire by the Germans in the summer of 1915.

Although his work on coordinating the Divisional artillery took him away from the front line, it is clear that Johnston enjoyed the logistical challenge of his work. His diary entries note some of these challenges in quite detailed terms, and he is critical of the work of some of his fellow officers in laying the necessary telephone lines. From his very first experience of combat at Mons, Johnston had seen how effective the German artillery could be. He recognised that to match the enemy, it was important to establish and maintain a good standard of communication between the artillery spotters in the front line and the gunners themselves behind the lines.

As a member of the Divisional Staff, Johnston was involved in the preparation of the assault on the Bellewarde Ridge in June of 1915. From the outset, Johnston saw that the attack was doomed to failure. Despite carrying out his work in his usual energetic manner, he could see that the artillery bombardment was woefully inadequate. His dairy describes the whole plan as "simply too wicked for words, and to my mind nothing short of murder..." He foresaw that the German artillery would lay down a heavy barrage on the packed front line trenches just before the troops went "over the top". His own Worcesters lost 13 officers and 250 men before the attack had even begun. On June 16th, the 3rd Division lost over 4000 men. It was, as Johnston himself reflected, a "useless waste of life".

As Christmas of 1915 drew near, Johnston was attached to the 9th Infantry Brigade as a Major, and true to style he immediately tried to ensure that his men received a hot Christmas meal. His festive goodwill did not extend to Sir John French, the Commander of the BEF, whose sacking he warmly welcomed.

More promotion followed. On New Year's Day, 1916, he heard that he was to be in charge of 25th Division's signalling. Johnston was irked by what he saw as a "poor job" in comparison to his post of Major, but he was now enough of a career soldier to recognise it for what it was – a "stepping stone" to future command posts. The plus factor about this promotion was that it took him away from the ever sodden trenches of Ypres, and he was now stationed near Vimy Ridge. Here, the trenches had been under French control, and his diaries are quick to point out the shortcomings of their handiwork. Near Mont St Eloi, he was disgusted to see unburied corpses lying out in the open, despite the fact that the sector was, after life around Ypres, really rather quiet.

On a training march behind the lines, he was accosted by a farmer in the village of Monchy Breton, who told him that they were the first English troops to march through the town since the Waterloo campaign of 1815. To prove his point, the farmer produced a letter to his great grandfather which had been written by the Commanding Officer of the 30th Regiment, apologising for the actions of some of his men when they were billeted in the village. Johnston's diary does not shed light on what these men did, although presumably the farmer's actions would have ensured that Johnston's men would be rather better guests.

One of the major features of this part of the front was the prevalence of mining operations. Johnston had experienced this frightening tactical development around Hill 60 near Ypres, but on the Vimy Ridge it became a daily threat to both sides. Troops nervously listened for sounds of digging. They would immediately evacuate the trench when the sounds stopped, as this was the likely signal for the charge that had been laid deep below them to be detonated. Such was the loss of life from these explosions that the front lines were only occupied by sentries in this part of the line. Johnston's men were expected to respond to the explosion by rushing forward to reach the lip of the newly blown crater as quickly as possible, and start digging in all over again.

He was on hand to witness this process on the morning of April 24th 1916, and led his men to the crater to fend off what he described as a rather half-hearted German assault. Some of the lines were within 30 yards of each other in this sector, and Johnston portrays the respective sentries peering over the lip of a huge crater, "watching each other like cats". His account may fill the modern day reader of his diaries with terror, and it is hard to imagine what it must have been like for any raw recruits, but this all-action, edgy scenario was clearly to Johnston's taste. In one German assault, Johnston went to the nearby Cheshire Regimental command post to see if he could get a sense of what was going on. Finding no officers present, Johnston crawled forward into the front line and joined in the action. He even picked up a rifle and began sniping. Again, Johnston refuses to play the stereotypical role of the high ranking First World War officer sheltering in a nearby chateau.

The rumours of a summer offensive had been growing throughout the first half of 1916, and Johnston's Division was moved south in preparation. He witnessed the huge artillery bombardment that signalled the opening of the "Big Show". Like Haig's planners, he thought that the German trenches would be completely destroyed by such a display. The events of July 1st were another sobering reminder that the Germans were a resourceful, professional foe. As his men were moved up from the reserve lines through Aveluy Wood for an attack on July 3rd, Johnston noted the strength and depth of the German dug outs.

His troops were making their way to the Leipzig Salient, a huge redoubt taken on July 1st by the men of the Highland Light Infantry. Now the Salient was the focal point for a continual barrage from the German artillery, as well as a series of determined counter attacks. Johnston's men were reinforcing this blood soaked piece of ground, and again, he was in the thick of the action. The site of the Leipzig Salient lies a few hundred yards to the south west of Lutyens' immense Memorial to the Missing at Thiepval, and the small quarry that formed the core of the German redoubt is now filled with trees and birdsong. During the course of the summer of 1916, however, it was a desperate scene, with both sides enduring terrible casualties as attack followed counter attack. Johnston describes it thus;

"When I got into the Leipzig Salient I found the place in a most awful state, the enemy's shelling was tremendous, trenches were obliterated and the rain helped to make what was left of them crumble away, dead dying and wounded were all over the place..."

After six days in the salient, his unit was moved to La Boisselle, another

19

strongpoint which had taken its toll of British troops on July 1st. Having survived the furious fighting and appalling conditions of the Leipzig Salient, it is interesting to note that even this battle hardened soldier was shocked by what he encountered at La Boisselle. "I have seen some bad places in this war but have seen nothing like this place," he comments on July 9th. He is also shocked by the incompetence of his superiors, who he describes as conducting affairs in this part of the line in a "most hopeless manner". After a fruitless night attack on Ovillers on July 14th, with the wholly predictable loss of 18 officers and 400 men, Johnston is moved to write that "some Staff officers ought to be hung for this."

Despite his willingness to be candid in his own diaries, Johnston was savvy enough to stay on the right side of the right people, and his career continued to progress. He was presented with the Croix de Guerre by one of the architects of July 1st, General Sir Hubert Gough, at a ceremony on August 27th, and on the following day he was given command of the 10th Cheshire Regiment.

The Somme campaign fizzled out in a sea of mud in November 1916, and Johnston's Cheshires were moved back to Flanders. His men were involved in the most famous mining operation of the war, the attack on the Messines Ridge in June of 1917. Nineteen mines, containing nearly a million tons of explosives, were detonated under the German front lines on the ridge, causing a shockwave that rattled the window frame in Lloyd George's study at Downing Street. The Cheshire's Commanding Officer was not able to witness the event, however. Much to his chagrin, his superiors blocked his request to move up into the front lines, nervous of losing a man of Johnston's quality and experience.

The focus of Haig's strategy had shifted north, away from the wrecked fields around the Somme, back to the Ypres sector. Encouraged by the success of the attack on Messines Ridge, the next "Big Push" was to north of Ypres, at the as yet little known village of Passchendaele. It sat on what appears to be, to the untrained eye, a slight rise in the ground. To Haig and his planners, it held the key to the conflict in this area. The higher ground had given the Germans the advantage for the past three years, and to move them off the ridge would strengthen the Allied hold on the Salient. Indeed, Haig felt that progress at this point in the line would lead on to a thrust that would enable his forces to go on to capture the Channel ports. Cynics who had survived the Somme campaign would remember that there were similarly extravagant claims made in the run up to July 1st.

As the Passchendaele campaign slithered to a muddy halt in the late summer rain, Johnston was put in charge of the 126th Infantry Brigade. In his diary extract for September 13th he describes himself as lucky to have landed such a post, but his luck was not to last. Presumably because he had no one immediately superior to him in the area, there was no one to tell him not to go out on his own impromptu reconnaissance missions, and he was shot through the leg by a sniper near the village of Sans Souci. The bone was shattered, and after being recovered in the middle of an artillery barrage by stretcher bearers, he was transferred to the main Dressing Station at Poperinghe. The first of several operations on his leg was carried out at the Casualty Clearing Station at Proven before he was sent back to England. On Christmas Day 1917 he was paid a visit by Queen Alexandria, and by April 1918, he was back home, his war over.

The modern reader of Johnston's diaries, whether in their original form held at the regimental museum in Worcester, or in Edwin Astill's edition published in 2007, would be shocked to discover that he was involved in the court martial and execution of six soldiers during the conflict. On the 23rd October 1914, he chaired the court martial of Private Edward Tanner of the Wiltshire Regiment.

Astill's book makes no reference to proceedings, with a gap left in the diary entries from the 21st to the 26th of October. Conspiracy theorists would, on checking Johnston's original diaries, discover that his entries on the days in question are distinctly neutral in tone. The day of the court martial, the 23rd, is described rather dismissively as a "slack day". Perhaps there is more subtext to be gleaned by the amateur psychologist from his throw away comment here – that the day gave him "no anxieties".

21

His apparent ability to divorce his own feelings from the events unfolding around him is highlighted in the summer of 1915. As previously mentioned, the attack on Bellewarde Farm to the west of Ypres in June 1915 had fizzled out, a failure predicted by Johnston. His anger at these events does flash through his account – he describes the attack as "nothing short of murder". As the Signalling Officer in charge, he had foreseen the potential for carnage as the 3rd Division troops were packed into front line trenches awaiting the order to go over the top. The four thousand casualties of that day, said Johnston, represented a "useless waste of life".

What the diary account does not tackle, however, is the shocking aftermath of the attack. On the 26th July, five members of his regiment, the 3rd Worcesters, were shot at dawn for desertion or cowardice in the face of the enemy. All five were executed near Ypres, and buried in different graveyards. Again, there is a gap in Astill's edition from July 21st to the 29th, and Johnston's original diary entries offer us no details as to what must have been an emotionally bruising few days. As with the Tanner case, Johnston makes no direct references to the events. Although he did not chair the court martial, it must have been a difficult time. The 3rd Worcesters were always "his" regiment. Whatever the circumstances, he would have felt the deaths of Privates Fellows, Hartells, Robinson and Thompson and Corporal Ives keenly. Does his silence in his diary entries reflect the fact that he felt that this was a "useless waste of life" too? Or is he embarrassed that "his" men had let the Regiment down?

On the 7th July, the day of his court martial, Johnston says he is "arranging one or two things". On the following day, the death penalty passed, Johnston has "a good deal of correspondence to settle up". The four privates were tried on the 14th of July, but Johnston's one line diary entry reads "Back at night to HQ doing office work etc. Very heavy rain in the morning."

On the lead up to the fateful day, Johnston seems to be busy, but wholly unconcerned. On the 18th July he says he "found a lot of things to arrange when I got back to the Ramparts but polished them off fairly quickly". He was back at the Ramparts in Ypres on the 20th to "sign papers and make various arrangements". On the very eve of the executions – and we need to be mindful of the fact that the shooting of these five men represents the single most extreme example of the imposition of capital punishment by the British Army in the whole war – Johnston's diary entry reads thus : "Polished off some office work and fixed up one or two things for tomorrow."

Was Johnston simply maintaining a business-like emotional distance from these events? Was it the sort of detachment expected of a high ranking (and ambitious) army man? Is it the deliberate neutrality of a professional soldier who saw what many at the time saw, that the maintenance of tough army discipline was central to fighting a war, and that these men were guilty, more than anything else, of "letting the side down"? These men had not "played up", they had given up.

From the outset of the war, Johnston had expected his men to show the qualities of bravery and teamwork, and was critical of those who fell short. "It makes one feel almost ill to see so many Englishmen being such cowards..." he commented during the retreat from Mons. At Neuve Chappelle in 1915, he was rallying the troops in the frontline in the face of German counterattacks, and also at one stage in the support trenches turning potential deserters back at the point of a gun. Although he acknowledges that these "poor devils" had been under murderous prolonged artillery bombardment, there is no doubt as to what he saw as the right thing to do.

The modern reader should be aware that even Johnston's account of the war has, in effect, been edited. He took on the task of writing up his notebooks during his convalescence. It may well be that these original notebooks would give us the missing pieces to this jigsaw. As Johnston copied them up in his careful, exact handwriting in the summer of 1918, he may have felt that a full blooded examination of these events would do no one any good. The wounds were too raw, and he had a career to build. Whatever the truth of the matter, there can be little doubt that as with all the 307 cases when men were taken out at dawn to be shot by their colleagues in the name of army discipline, it is far easier for us, a century later, to make judgements.

Depressingly, another member of the 3rd Worcester Regiment was shot at dawn two years later. Sgt. J.T. Wall was executed on the 6th September 1917 for desertion in the face of the enemy. Even more depressingly, he was fighting over the same ground, on the Bellewarde Ridge outside Ypres. For Johnston, it was a "quiet day". By this time, Johnston was in charge of the 10th Cheshires, and had warned Private Ernest Bryant, a deserter who had been captured at Boulogne, that the Battalion was due to go into action again. Tragically, Bryant did not heed the warning, and was executed at Bethune for desertion on the 27th October, 1917. By this time, the sniper's bullet had ended Johnston's war, and he was in the middle of a series of operations on his shattered leg.

On his recovery from these operations he was sent to the Rhineland for the early part of the 1919 cricket season, but his leg injury meant that his first class cricket career was all but over. The litany of surgical procedures had left him with one leg four inches shorter than the other, which necessitated the use of a runner when he batted. It certainly meant the end of his occasional leg break bowling. Johnston played his last match for Hampshire at the end of June, scoring 37 and 36 not out batting at the top of the order against Gloucestershire. His last first class match was as part of the Gentlemen's XI playing a Combined Services side at Lord's. Perhaps significantly, he was dismissed by being run out. He continued to play invitational matches throughout the 1920's, ending his last match for the MCC at Lords with an innings of 96 against the Royal Engineers.

Johnston worked his way towards retirement from the Army in 1937, becoming the Chief Education Officer at the Royal Military College along the way. The outbreak of war in 1939 meant that he was drafted back into uniform, working in the Army general staff at Aldershot, and spending some time working with the Foreign Office's Political Intelligence Department. Alex Johnston died on the 17th of October 1952, aged 68.

Arthur Jaques

The Pas de Calais in Northern France has rarely enjoyed very much in the way of popularity. Inside the country, the people are often cruelly stereotyped as ignorant, their "Cht'i" accents mocked by the chic Parisiens and the cosmopolitan Southerners. Tourists flash through this landscape with barely a glance, their eyes fixed on the tarmac of the Autoroute des Anglais that leads them to the ski pistes of the Savoie, or the lavender fields of Provence. The slag heaps near Bethune hardly encourage the casual tourist to stop.

This flat plain, dotted as it is with evidence of its industrial activity, is part of what Richard Holmes called the "Fatal Avenue" of Europe. Its topography has, from medieval times, encouraged kings, dictators and generals to consider it to be prime battlefield real estate. The roads of Artois and Flanders have borne the weight of troops fighting across the centuries. A different and less fussy brand of tourist.

And so it was when the B.E.F. arrived in the late summer of 1914. As the Western Front trenches snaked their way north from the chalk uplands around Arras and dropped down into the coalfields around Lens the British troops saw that they were into working class territory. Squat, red brick terraces in small towns dominated by pit head gear and slag heaps. Those troops who had escaped the mines of Yorkshire or the North East may have wondered if they were abroad at all.

 After a series of failed offensives in the spring of 1915, this was to be the focal point for another "Big Push" in the autumn. General Haig, when asked to look at the plans for an offensive in the area, said that he was of the opinion that the ground was "not favourable for an attack". The open nature of the land, with open stretches of No Man's Land in front of the fortified hills and villages meant that the German machine guns would make a frontal infantry assault a potentially disastrous undertaking. Sadly, Haig's initial assessment was to prove right.

The Loos Memorial to the Missing is situated on the old German front line on the straight road that links Bethune and Lens. The memorial is built on top of the old German redoubt, which became known as "Dud Corner" because of the discarded shells that littered this part of the road after the war. It was calculated that approximately a third of the 366,000 shells fired by the British 18 pounder guns at Loos failed to detonate, so it is not surprising that "duds" continue to turn up in the ploughed fields all around here every year.

The steps up to the tower in the northern corner of the building takes the tourist up to a platform, which is as good a place as any to get a view of the battlefield. In this exposed spot, the ever present breeze might remind you that Haig planned the first Allied use of poison gas in this area. This new and dreadful weapon had been used by the Germans in Ypres. As novices in the "art" of this new form of warfare, there was considerable nervousness about the role it had to play in the offensive. The men did not enjoy sharing their front line trenches with the deadly canisters. Haig had high hopes that it would give him the breakthrough that the other offensives of 1915 had singularly failed to deliver. The success of the gas attack depended on the wind direction, and the final decision on that was taken on Haig's order – he asked one of his subalterns to light a cigarette and blow some smoke. A qualified meteorologist might have been able to tell him that the wind was not strong enough, nor consistent enough in terms of direction, to form the basis for such a crucial move. When released, the gas cloud did as much damage to the Allied attackers as it did to the Germans. The hopes of a breakthrough drifted away on the wind too.

There is also a good view to the north of Mazingarbe, a wrecked village behind the Allied lines in the autumn of 1915. It enjoyed a grisly reputation, as eleven soldiers were executed there during the war. From the viewing platform the battlefield tourist can see to the east exactly what Haig feared. There is no cover. The eye travels along the ploughed furrows towards the distant horizon. Even the agriculture here feels industrial. In 1915 the killing certainly was, with the British troops suffering some 60,000 casualties for next to no gain. With the French attacking the area around Vimy Ridge, away to the south, the British High Command was in a position where it had to be seen to be supporting their allies. Kitchener admitted that "we may suffer very heavy losses" when he visited Sir John French, the Commander of the B.E.F., but the Secretary for War made it clear that the attack would have to take place.

The steps down from the viewing platform take you into the enclosed cemetery, which is flanked on three sides by stone panels which list the names of over 20,000 men who have no known grave after the conflicts in this immediate area of the front. There are a further 684 named graves in the cemetery, with a high proportion of Scottish troops. The Battle of Loos became known as the "Scottish Somme".

On the panel dedicated to the West Yorkshire regiment, there are two brothers named, both lost as their unit attacked the area known as "Bois Hugo". The Jaques brothers were officers, two of the sixteen lost from just one battalion on Sunday 27th September, 1915. Three hundred other ranks became casualties as this attempt to capture the high ground beyond the village of Loos floundered in the face of the deadly German crossfire. The Jaques brothers had lived at Red Lodge, in Bassett, Southampton. Arthur Jaques, the younger of the two, had very recently married, and had been one of the stars of the 1914 County cricket season.

Despite his height, Jaques took a while to get noticed in cricketing terms. By the time he made his considerable impact on the County scene, he was already into his mid twenties. A look at the archives will show that success did not come easily to him. He made his debut for Aldenham School in May of 1904 in a match against St John's Leatherhead. The school's established bowling attack meant that he played the junior role so well known to cricketing folk – he did not bowl, and batted well down the order. In his first innings for the school in the next match against Merchant Taylor's he failed to score.

Jaques finally made an impact by taking a catch in the game against Forest School, and he was rewarded with promotion up the batting order. He responded with a score of 22 not out. Arthur must have felt that he had arrived, that he had proved a point to his elder team mates. He was still to bowl a ball, however.

Jaques had to wait until the 1905 season before making that breakthrough. He took his first school wicket in a game against Highgate School, and then removed three of the top four Merchant Taylor's School batsmen. Now, he was clearly seen as a key player. The coach even trusted Jaques with the No.3 batting spot, although he struggled that season to justify that aspect of his selection.

His seam bowling, however, continued to develop. On the 1st of June 1907 against Highgate he took nine wickets in an innings. Later that month he finally rewarded the coach's faith in his batting ability by scoring a half century against Mill Hill School.

On leaving school, it is interesting to note that like his eventual County colleague Lionel Tennyson he did not make an impact in University cricket. He played at club level for Trojans back in Hampshire, and appears in the 1911 census as living (presumably lodging, or perhaps visiting on that particular day) at a house in Poole. Under "Employment" he is entered in the records as being of "Private Means". Whatever the source of these means, it had freed him up to play cricket. So it was that by this unusual route Jaques came to the notice of the MCC, and he made his first class debut in Barbados on their West Indian tour. In cricketing terms his performances there were pretty ordinary, but the experience seems to have stoked his sense of ambition, and brought him to the notice of the Hampshire selectors.

He was on tour again in May 1911 – this time in Ireland with Hampshire. He scored 46 in a hefty Hampshire score of 449 all out at College Park against Dublin University, but wealth of bowling options meant that Jaques only bowled five overs. He had to wait another two years before making his County debut at the County Ground against Derbyshire. He produced a quietly effective all round performance, taking two wickets and managing to score 22 runs in a lowly score of 159 all out.

Of his breakthrough 1913 season Altham wrote in the *Hampshire Cricket History* - "A useful recruit to our attack this year was found in Arthur Jaques: long-armed and tall, with the ability to swerve the ball into the batsman at a fastish medium pace, he showed promising control of length and stamina."

Soon he was trusted with the new ball. It would have been quite a moment for the young man, standing at the end of his run up, waiting to bowl the ball that would start the game. He was in a team that was not short of front line options - Kennedy, Newman and Brown were all looking on. The Hampshire tactics were favouring the use of Kennedy and Newman in tandem, with Jaques asked to produce a tight opening spell to threaten the openers. The pressure was on him to perform, but he seems to have been at ease with the task that his captain had set him, and quickly established himself in the team.

Jaques played against Warwickshire at the end of May 1913, and would have admired the fluid action of another one of English cricket's rising stars – Percy Jeeves. The Warwickshire medium pacer took four of the top five Hampshire wickets in the first innings at the County Ground. Jeeves was also building himself quite a reputation, and the cricket mad writer Wodehouse named his most famous character after him. Tragically, Jeeves was killed in the summer of 1916, attacking High Wood, one of the most notorious killing grounds on the blood soaked Somme battlefield.

A five wicket haul against a strong Kent batting line up showed that his inswinging seamers could trouble any batsman. He backed up this performance with 5 – 61 off 30 overs against Worcestershire at the County Ground. Jaques removed the top four opposition batsmen for scores of 0, 3, 9 and 1. This match was Cecil Abercrombie's county debut, and Hampshire followers must have seen a bright future with these two young additions to the batting and bowling resources of the County.

An analysis of Arthur Jaques' bowling figures shows that Hampshire's new bowling star showed a veteran's control of line and length – never easy when bowling inswinging deliveries, particularly on a batsman-friendly surface such as the County Ground. The Essex batsmen could only score seven runs off his eight nagging overs at the end of July 1913, and they lost two wickets in the process. But as any bowler will attest, it is not all about keeping the runs down, and Jaques would have felt elated to get to 50 wickets for the season in the first week of August.

He was also beginning to show the sort of batting prowess that had seen him promoted up the order in junior cricket teams. A score of 27 in a low scoring match at Cheltenham, followed by 47 not out against Sussex would have had the young bowler dreaming of the "genuine all rounder" tag.

When the long hot summer of 1914 came round, Jaques was eager to build on his promising debut season. He was to be ever present in the Hampshire side, opening the campaign with 5-31 off 14 overs against Leicestershire – his best figures to date. Jaques' control of swing and seam movement made him a real threat on early season wickets, and he took four wickets against the powerful Yorkshire side. One of his victims was the England player Roy Kilner, a man who was to miss the opening attack of the Leeds Pals on the Somme by virtue of a wound that he picked up from a stray shell as he made his way up the communication trench to the front line. Bearing in mind that there were 528 Leeds Pals lost in the attack, Kilner can be counted a lucky man. Because he was a right handed bowler, the wound to his left hand did not stop him from representing his country after the war.

In his next match, at May's Bounty in Basingstoke, Jaques destroyed the Derbyshire batting line up by taking eight wickets in the first innings. It was a match-winning performance. Once again, it is important to note the economical run rate. Eight wickets for sixty seven runs off thirty overs. Just to rub salt into Derbyshire's wounds, Jaques took six wickets in the second innings.

A five wicket haul against Gloucestershire at the United Services Ground in Portsmouth showed that he was in a rich vein of form. Whatever surface he was asked to bowl on, Jaques was proving to be the sort of bowler the opening batsmen feared. His nagging control of length and swing would tax the soundest of defences. He was also quick enough to threaten with the short ball, and Hampshire cricket historian H.S. Altham credited him with being one of the pioneers of what came to be known as "leg theory". Hampshire fielders would pressurise the opposition openers with catchers close in on the leg side, and Jaques would bowl a line and length that would later gain notoriety in the game as "Bodyline". Jaques reached the significant milestone of 100 County wickets in the match against Nottinghamshire on June 10th 1914. The future looked bright.

He was up to 50 wickets for the season in his next match, when he and Kennedy ripped the Somerset batting to shreds at the Rec in Bath. Jaques took 6-33 as the home team subsided to a miserable 83 all out. After the Hampshire batsmen made a score of 313 in their innings, the Somerset players ran up the white flag in their second turn at the crease. They were bowled out for just 38 runs, with Jaques helping himself to eight wickets at a cost of just 21 runs.

Cricket, more than any other sport, will soon remind you that it's not meant to be easy all of the time. Sometimes you have to go through more difficult experiences – to enjoy the highs you have to get through the lows. In such prime form, Jaques would have opened the bowling against Surrey on the 18th June 1914 feeling on top of the cricketing world. The ball seemed to be obeying his every whim, and his name would have been raised in discussions between County opening batsmen up and down the country. One such batsman was the young Jack Hobbs. Jaques came face to face (or ball to bat) with one of the cricketing greats. Hobbs scored 163 runs, and Jaques bowled 33 overs in an effort to dislodge him. It is probably significant that Hampshire tried eight different bowlers during his innings, all to no avail, however, as he passed 1000 runs for the season. The Great War robbed cricket of some talent, and in the case of Jack Hobbs it robbed the cricketing public of four years of a quite exceptional batsman at the top of his game.

After the chastening experience of bowling to Jack Hobbs in full flow, it is to Jaques' credit that he bounced back with strong performances against Worcestershire at the County Ground, where his "genuine all rounder" dreams were re-awakened with a score of 68 as he batted with Kennedy to frustrate the tired opposition bowlers. In the return fixture at Tipton Road in Dudley, the two sides allowed the match to fizzle out in a high scoring draw. News had reached the ground that in a distant Balkan country, someone called the Archduke Franz Ferdinand had been assassinated. A cloud was cast over proceedings, but at that moment no one could quite comprehend what was to come next. The Balkan crisis developed, and the air was heavy with talk of war as the sun continued to shine into August. Jaques took eleven wickets in the match against Warwickshire in August, and reached the 100 wickets for the season mark. By this stage, however, British army boots were on the ground in France and Belgium, and the cricketing feats of Hampshire's young tyro were barely registering a by-line in the newspapers. Arthur Jaques ended his season, and his cricketing career, with 6 – 55 off 23 overs at Dean Park, Bournemouth.

Having gained commissions in the 12th West Yorkshire Regiment, the Jaques brothers would have undergone training in the Home Counties. The West Yorkshires were part of the 21st Division, which was based near Tring. June 1915 saw them at Halton Park, where they were finally issued with rifles. Soon they were on the move, this time to the camp at Witley. Lord Kitchener inspected them on manoeuvres on 12th August. The losses incurred by the B.E.F. in the failed campaigns of 1915 meant that the 21st Division was soon sending advance parties over the Channel, and the remainder of the Division left for France from Folkestone on the 7th of September. The different units gathered at a camp near the town of Tilques.

A sense of excitement must have been building by this time, but the worsening weather, allied to a series of taxing forced marches, would have tested that early enthusiasm. The men were marching ten to fifteen miles a night, carrying heavy packs in pouring rain. Exhausted and soaked to the skin, they would be allowed to rest at daybreak, and lay down in the mud by the side of the road. It was up to officers such as Arthur to keep these troops moving and following orders. This would have been no mean feat when the men discovered two days out of Loos that their food supplies had not caught up with them.

One of the great mistakes made at the Battle of Loos was that reserve units such as the 12th Yorkshires were kept too far back from the front. The modest gains of the initial attacks were then lost as German counter attacks wrestled back control of their trenches before Allied reserve units could help to consolidate the ground taken. So it was that the 12th Yorkshires did not get into action until Sunday 27th September. For such inexperienced troops, the sloping ground near Bois Hugo became a killing ground. With most of their officers (including Arthur and Joseph Jaques) dead, the remainder of the men crawled back to their frontline trenches. The 21st Division had suffered 3,800 casualties. No ground was gained. It was the final nail in the coffin for Sir John French, who was sacked as Commander-in-Chief of the B.E.F. shortly afterwards.

According to one report by Major-General Forester-Walker the 12th West Yorkshires did not behave with credit and retired without due cause. When one looks at the shortcomings of the planning and execution of the Battle of Loos, it is easy to see why men such as Forester-Walker were so quick to play the blame game. Inexperienced, exhausted and hungry, Jaques and his men found out exactly what Haig meant when he talked about "unfavourable ground". For one young officer in the Royal Welsh, it was his first taste of combat. Robert Graves describes Loos as a "bloody balls-up". A hundred years later, looking out from the viewing platform at the Memorial, one instinctively trusts the judgement of the inexperienced officer over the Major-General.

Cecil Abercrombie

In 1977, a battered, dust covered photo album was picked out of a builder's skip on a street in central London. The contents were beguiling enough to make the rescuer pause, and the album was saved. The photographs inside transported the viewer to a sepia tinted world of posed Edwardian elegance, although the identity of these figures from the past was initially a complete mystery. Eventually, it was discovered that one of the central characters in the mystery was Cecil Abercrombie. A rugby international and, all too briefly, a Hampshire cricketer, Abercrombie was killed serving at sea at the Battle of Jutland at the end of May, 1916.

Cecil Halliday Abercrombie was born on the 12th of April 1886, the son of son of Walter D Abercrombie of the Indian Police Force. His mother, Kate, was from another Colonial family, the von Bimbras. The Abercrombies lived in Muzufferpore, and the political sensitivies of working in this part of the Empire may explain why the decision was made to send Cecil to school in England. He attended Harlington Manor in Torrington, Berkshire from 1893 until 1900. His name appears on the census of 1901 as a boarder at Berkhampstead School, but by this time Royal Navy lists show him to have signed up as a cadet at Dartmouth in the autumn of 1900. Presumably Cecil was finishing off his education there because he could not be a full time sailor as yet. Berkhampstead would have been happy to accommodate the young cadet, albeit for a short time, as he was developing into a serious all round sporting talent.

By 1902, Abercrombie was at sea, firstly as a midshipman on a cruiser called *Highflyer*, then on her sister ship, *Hyacinth*. He was part of the most powerful naval force in the world. Indeed, its power was such that the ambitious Kaiser realised that Germany would have to beef up its own naval resources if his country was to challenge for its "place in the sun". The Kaiser's own mother noted that "Wilhelm's one idea is to have a navy which shall be larger and stronger than the British navy". In 1898 the German Fleet Act turned his ambition into steel. British naval supremacy, which had been assumed for most of the nineteenth century, was now seriously challenged. New German ships were being launched with menacing regularity in the early years of the new century. Jackie Fisher, the First Sea Lord, put his faith in the revolutionary new 'Dreadnought' battleships, but feared that Britain would still not keep pace with German industrial power. The jingoistic press in Britain stirred up the debate, calling for more of the new 'Dreadnought' class ships to be built in retaliation. The cry of "We want eight and we won't wait," ensured that the politicians swam along with this rising tide of public opinion. It was in this febrile climate that Abercrombie's early naval career was played out. The twentieth century was going to be a great time to be an arms manufacturer.

The young midshipman Abercrombie was given a taste of the imperial dimensions of the Navy's reach when *Hyacinth* was sent to patrol the waters of east Africa. The Dervish forces under the Mullah were also threatening the Empire, and the British forces teamed up with the Italians, the other Western interest in the region. Both parties decided that the port of Ilig in Somaliland was a key concern, as it was being used as a supply route for the Mullah's army. Rear Admiral Hood gathered a combined force of approximately 750 men from the three ships in the taskforce – the *Hyacinth*, *Fox* and *Mohawk* – as well as some accompanying troops from the Hampshire Regiment. He led the landing party in a night attack on a beach that was guarded by some Dervishes, and after overcoming this force, attacked the port from inland.

The operation was a complete success, Hood suffering only nine casualties. Abercrombie, a teenager, had been involved. Quite how he felt as they rowed towards unknown enemy forces on a darkened beach can only be imagined. Like other members of the landing party he was awarded the Africa Services Medal. Hood gained the Distinguished Service Order. The Spectator magazine said that the whole affair had been "excellently managed, and the gallantry of the storming party is specially commended".

As the first Dreadnought battleship made its entry into the Solent from Portsmouth, Cecil Abercrombie learnt of his promotion to Acting Sub-Lieutenant. His name appears on a list of those attending a Sub-Lieutenant's training course at Greenwich in the spring of that year. By the summer of 1907 he was a full Lieutenant, serving on *Irresistible*. By this time he was playing rugby for United Services RFC at Portsmouth, his strength and athleticism making him a formidable loose forward. Surviving pictures show him to have been an imposing specimen, and he would not have looked out of place in modern rugby's highly trained, carefully sculpted squads. Cecil was picked to play representative rugby for the Navy side, and played against the touring Wallabies in 1908.

His qualities soon attracted the attention of the Scottish selectors. He made his international debut in 1910 in front of 12,000 raucous fans at the Balmoral Showground in Belfast as part of a victorious Scottish side who beat the hosts 14 – nil. Abercrombie went on to play for Scotland on six occasions between 1910 and 1913. The high point of his international rugby career came at the Stade Olympique Yves-du-Manoir in Colombes, in the Five Nations match against the French side on 2nd January 1911. France won an exciting contest 16 – 15, but Abercrombie's name appeared on the scoreboard. The game itself was a watershed moment for French rugby, representing as it does the first ever victory of Equipe de France in the Championship. Before the game kicked off, the French were scanning the crowd for a fifteenth player, with Vareilles of Stade Francais having inexplicably failed to show up. The named substitute, Antoine Franquenelle, was late, having missed his train at St Lazare. The French team manager spotted a familiar face in the crowd, Laffite from the Bordeaux club, and urged him to play. Laffite was in the process of changing his military uniform for some borrowed kit when Monsieur Franquenelle turned up, presumably already warmed up by a brisk jog from the station. Abercrombie and his team mates were accused of being too over-confident on the day, but that would be understandable in the context of these events before kick-off.

His all-round sporting prowess aided his naval career too, as he became the ship's "India Rubber Man", in charge of Physical Training on board. In 1911 he attended the School of Physical Training, and was drafted onto two training ships at Dartmouth – the *Fishguard* and then the *Pomone* – which gave Cecil an opportunity to train cadets in the finer points of what was then known as "muscle bending". It may be that this opportunity allowed him to play even more sport himself, as he begins to emerge as a serious cricketer. He represented the Navy, Cecil quickly gaining a reputation as a hard hitting middle order batsman. His natural strength and sense of timing, particularly off the front foot, could wreak havoc. He also bowled effective right arm medium pace, his height creating awkward bounce on any helpful wickets. The added time spent on land in his PT work would have allowed him to hone these skills.

Abercrombie does not make an appearance in the 1912 rugby Championship, and it is not clear if this was due to the whims of the selectors, injury, or naval commitments. It may be that he was on board his new ship *Defence* as she sailed to the China station. In the summer of 1912, however, he was able to play some cricket, impressing the crowd at Lords with some destructive hitting in the Army v Navy match. He scored freely, with his century in the second innings featuring a big six that landed on the players' dressing room balcony. Even by today's standards, with players wielding heavy bats that would be considered quite a feat. His century was completed in just 130 minutes, with twelve boundaries, and he had also taken four wickets in the match. It is important to remember that these Forces games drew big crowds, as they loomed large in the nation's sporting calendar, so Abercrombie's exploits put him in the spotlight. It may well be that it was this performance that drew the attention of the Hampshire committee. One Hampshire player, Alec Johnston, would have heard from his Army colleagues about what it was like to try to stop the flow of cover drives from Cecil's bat.

It is particularly poignant to note the events of 1913, representing as it does Cecil Abercrombie's "annus mirabilis". On the 1st of February he was called in to the Scottish rugby side to play at Inverleith. A strong Welsh side overcame their hosts 8 – nil and it was to be Cecil Abercrombie's last cap. It may be that as he was just entering his thirtieth year that this was inevitable, particularly as his cricketing career seemed to offer more longevity, and perhaps now even greater prospects. More poignant still, however, is to reflect on the fact that of the fifteen players appearing for Scotland on that day, nine of them were to perish in the war. Scottish rugby lost more players than any other home nation. Of the 89 international players lost by the forces of the Empire (the Home Nations, plus Australia and New Zealand), 30 of them were Scottish, with the London Scottish club accounting for 17 of that figure.

On referencing Abercrombie in its section on War Deaths, *Wisden* notes that "...his fame rests on what he accomplished in a single season." And what a season it was. The carnage he had created in the second innings at

Lords in 1912 gave his Hampshire employers an idea that they were bringing in a player of considerable potential, but even they must have been stunned by the return on their investment. In just 13 matches in the summer of 1913, Abercrombie scored nearly a thousand runs. In his very first match, he scored 126 against Oxford University at Southampton's County Ground. The match against the Army in 1912 had been his debut in First Class cricket, and in the first few days of July 1913 he must have been tempted to think that this was an easy game. Although he was dismissed fairly cheaply in his next two matches against Worcestershire at Southampton and Essex at his old stamping ground at the United Services ground in Portsmouth, Cecil was a fireworks display just waiting to happen.

The fuse was lit in no uncertain terms at his first away match. Hampshire travelled to Dudley for a return match against Worcestershire. The included another talented striker of the ball in their eleven in their line-up – His Lordship Lionel Tennyson made his debut, and contributed solid runs at number three in the batting line up. But his debut was overshadowed by Abercrombie's heroics. With the Hampshire first innings fizzling out, Hamilton Smith, the very model of a modern tail ender, came to join Cecil in the middle. Both men clearly decided to have some fun, and the pair produced a century stand for the final wicket. Cecil scored 144 runs in just 135 minutes, an innings that featured 17 fours and a six. There was even an all run 5 on the scorecard – which would have been all in a day's work for the PT instructor, but it is not recorded what number eleven Smith felt about that particular moment.

The return game away to Essex at Leyton was next on the fixture list at the end of July, and Hampshire were under pressure from the outset. The home side amassed over 500 runs in their first innings, with three of their batsman scoring centuries. Hampshire scrambled to 190 all out in reply, and had to bat again. The omens were not good. Abercrombie, their hero at Dudley, had been dismissed tamely for just five runs. In the second innings, however, Tennyson scored a maiden century for the county, and this lifted the players around him. Abercrombie then combined with

George Brown to produce a mammoth stand of 325 for the seventh wicket, a record that still stands today. Abercrombie contributed 165, including 11 fours and 4 sixes. It was a draw that would have felt like a victory.

The veteran England and Yorkshire all rounder Wilf Rhodes seems to have had this new batting sensation sorted out, however. He dismissed Cecil twice, including a duck in the first innings in Hampshire's next match at Harrogate. The Yorkshire team featured two men who joined the Leeds Pals in the following year. Kilner was wounded before going over the top on the first day of the Somme campaign, and was back at a Casualty Station as Booth and 969 other Leeds Pals attacked the German lines at Serre. Only 70 Pals were able to answer the roll call that night. The Yorkshire cricketer Booth was not amongst them. He had shared a house with his sisters, and they left his bedroom as it was, lighting a candle there every night in his name.

Abercrombie was stifled by the bowlers for much of August, with Hampshire struggling against Middlesex and Gloucestershire, but an improved performance against Sussex coincided with Abercrombie getting good starts and was promoted to the top of the order in the second innings. This return to the exceptional form of July was bad news for the bowlers of Somerset. Back at the United Services ground, the Hampshire team imposed itself on the Westcountrymen from the outset, with George Brown's five wicket haul reducing them to 158 all out. Abercrombie top scored with 79 belligerent runs after four of the top five Hampshire batsmen failed to make double figures, and this innings proved to be the game's watershed moment. In the second innings he had the satisfaction of helping Philip Mead polish off the hundred runs that his team needed to win the game by the comfortable margin of seven wickets.

The last game of Abercrombie's season – and, indeed, his life – was played against Gloucestershire at Dean Park, Bournemouth, on 28th August, 1913. The world was only a year from the great cataclysm that was to sweep Abercrombie and so many others away, but the Hampshire batting line up gave their supporters some indicators of what might be. Abercrombie played in a typically robust manner for his score of 65 in the first innings, but there were other dangerous players in that team. Lionel Tennyson gave another good performance at number three, giving his usual impression of a man with other appointments to attend to that day. Sandwiched between his brisk 83 and Abercrombie's knock was a solid fifty by Philip Mead. Always happy to play second fiddle to the swashbucklers, Mead was developing a reputation on the circuit as an extremely difficult man to dismiss. His 171 in the Hampshire second innings ensured that Abercrombie's cricketing career ended on a note of triumph.

Hampshire's supporters would have been licking their lips at the prospect of this middle order dismantling County attacks in the 1914 season, but naval duty called for Abercrombie. His ship *Defence* was moved to the Mediterranean, and he was based in Malta. The photo album that was rescued from the London skip showed a series of snaps of Cecil and his wife Cecily blissfully enjoying themselves. In the summer of 1914, said Leon Trotsky, "History had already poised its gigantic soldier's boot over the anthill" in Europe, but there is no sense of concern here as the young couple posed in the sun. But as a Lieutenant on the flagship for the First Cruiser Squadron, however, Cecil would have been worried. Anglo-German relations were in a tailspin, and if the countries were to go to war, the young Lieutenant would have been fully aware of how critical the naval struggle would be.

Admiral John Jellicoe, the Admiral of the Fleet who had successfully lobbied for the ramping up of the "Dreadnought" programme, was known as the man who could lose a war in an afternoon. The balance of power still favoured the British Fleet in the summer of 1914, but the destructive capabilities of modern ships meant that naval tactics were inevitably cagey. One such modern ship was the German cruiser *Goeben*, which was loose in the Mediterranean with the *Breslau* as war was declared. The British Cruiser Fleet's commander, Sir Ernest Troubridge, had spent some time as an observer during the Russo-Japanese War a decade earlier. His gunnery officer, Fawcett Wray, advised him that the *Goeben*'s eleven inch guns easily outranged anything that the British Fleet had to offer, so a prolonged game of cat and mouse developed in the Mediterranean as Troubridge tried to outmanoeuvre his German counterpart, Admiral Wilhelm Souchon.

The Admiralty was determined to stop the *Goeben* and *Breslau* from joining up with the Austro-Hungarian Fleet in the northern Adriatic. More importantly, Troubridge was charged with the task of keeping the German raiders away from the Dardanelles, as there was the distinct threat that the Turks would be able to give them a strategically important home port.

Despite the numerical advantage in terms of ships at Troubridge's disposal – including Abercrombie's *Defence* – the Goeben's superior arms and armour meant that he decided against a direct confrontation. On the night of the 6th-7th August, Abercrombie and his colleagues were forced to give up the chase. Troubridge sent a message to the Admiralty at 0449hrs:
"Being only able to meet *Goeben* outside the range of our guns and inside his, I have abandoned the chase with my squadron. *Goeben* evidently going to the Eastern Mediterranean."

The German ships had escaped, and headed east. They were turned over to the Ottoman fleet, and Turkey's entry into the war on Germany's side hinted at the fact that was a scenario that had already been discussed in the corridors of government in Berlin and Istanbul. Opinion was divided on Troubridge's decision. Churchill, as First Lord of the Admiralty, was furious, claiming that Sir Ernest had not been following orders when he avoided a battle. Troubridge and his supporters said that he had been right to avoid a fight where the odds would have favoured the German ships. Fawcett Wray, alongside Troubridge on the bridge on that evening, had been moved to tears by his superior's dilemma. "Sir, this is the bravest thing you have ever done," he said, but the outrage over the event led to both men having to stand in front of a Court Martial. Although the case was dismissed, their careers were effectively over.

No doubt Abercrombie and his fellow officers shared some of Churchill's frustration at Sir Ernest's failure to engage the *Goeben*. They were eager to earn their spurs, and Abercrombie may have reflected on the contrast with the decisive leadership shown by his commanders back in Africa, his only direct experience of combat thus far. At the same time, he was an experienced enough naval man to understand Troubridge's dilemma. The *Defence* was an older ship, dangerously close to picking up the "obsolete" tag. She would have succumbed to the firepower of the *Goeben*, and in turn would have been unable to pierce her armour. The officers on the *Defence* would have been all too aware of that fact.

They would have been keen to "do their bit" to make up for this ignominious start, but the naval "phoney war" lasted for several months for Abercrombie and his colleagues. After spending a month patrolling the Dardanelles, they received an order at the start of September to join Cradock's force as it hunted down Von Spee's Cruiser squadron. The order was reversed, and *Defence* turned back towards the Mediterranean. In October, they were told to join Cradock again. By the time they reached Montevideo, however, on the 3rd of November 1914, Von Spee had sunk two British cruisers, *Good Hope* and *Monmouth*, and Cradock himself was dead. *Defence* had missed the Battle of Coronel.

The frustration of those on board would not have been helped by the order that sent the ship to South Africa. Whilst they were steaming across the South Atlantic, Von Spee's force was cornered and defeated at the Falkland Islands. The *Defence* was left with the unglamorous task of accompanying a troopship from Cape Town to England. On arrival, Abercrombie and his fellow seamen learned that they were to join the Grand Fleet in Scapa Flow.

Defence became the flagship for Rear Admiral Sir Robert Arbuthnot's 1st Cruiser Squadron. Arbuthnot was, like Cecil, a rugby player from the ranks of the United Services club in Portsmouth, and he had a reputation as a fearless, if occasionally rash, character. An ex-boxer, he used to challenge his dinner guests to some gentle post prandial sparring and a fight with some of his own sailors at one port left two of his charges in hospital. The naval historian Andrew Gordon goes as far as to describe him as "in a colloquial if not a clinical sense, insane". It would have been made clear to the crew of the *Defence* that Arbuthnot would not pass up on an opportunity to engage with the enemy, as Troubridge had done.

Throughout 1915, however, the German Imperial Fleet was bottled up in port, unable to risk a full on confrontation with Jellicoe. Again, a sense of the "phoney war" settled on the respective naval forces. Occasional forays from home ports were rare. On the German side, there was the fear of being outnumbered and overpowered by the Jellicoe's forces. Jellicoe himself was defensively minded. His Fleet was superior – why risk a battle where that superiority could be lost?

By the spring of 1916, however, it became clear to the Germans that the blockade created by British Naval superiority had to be challenged. Admiral Reinhard Scheer recognised that the status quo would not change in one huge battle, but worked on trying to manoeuvre Jellicoe's forces into a battle where he could begin to make inroads into Britain's numerical superiority. Raids on east coast towns such as Lowestoft failed to draw Jellicoe's Grand Fleet out into the open, so a plot was hatched to engage Vice Admiral David Beatty's Cruiser Fleet in the North Sea. Unfortunately for Scheer, however, the German code had been broken early in the war. Jellicoe knew that a trap was being set. On May 30th, 1916, Beatty's Cruiser Fleet left British waters, heading for a meeting point off the coast of the Danish island of Jutland where, unbeknown to Scheer, he would be joined by Jellicoe's Grand Fleet.

For sailors on both sides this was "Der Tag" – The Day they had been waiting for. All the training, the theorising, the months of waiting in port was finally at an end. The vast destructive potential of their ships was a palpable shock to them all, however. The latest class of British super Dreadnoughts were firing shells weighing in at 1,920 pounds, and in the late afternoon of May 31st ships from both sides began to find out what this sort of firepower could do to steel and human flesh. The early exchanges did not go well for the British force – as he watched the *Queen Mary* and the *Indefatigable* sink, and fires raged on his own flagship, the *Lion*, Beatty famously turned to his fellow officers and said, "There seems to be something wrong with our bloody ships today."

Crucially, however, Beatty's "run to the north" was bringing Jellicoe and the Grand Fleet into play. As the two main fleets converged, Abercrombie's ship, the *Defence,* was placed between these bigger, more powerful ships. Rear Admiral Sir R K Arbuthnot, in charge of *Defence* was not overawed by the prospect, and his actions that day do not seem to have taken into consideration the fact that his ship would most likely come off second best in a fire fight against a more modern opponent. He altered his course, a move that could have resulted in a catastrophic collision with Beatty had the bigger ship not taken evasive action. Most annoyingly for the Vice Admiral, *Defence* now obscured his view of the main German force. Arbuthnot was heading straight for the first German ship to come into view, the stricken *SMS Wiesbaden*. He believed that his ship, together with *Warrior* could easily sink the disabled German cruiser, which had been earlier torpedoed by the destroyer *Onslow*. However, as *Defence* closed on *Wiesbaden*, the German battle cruisers and battleships of III Squadron appeared out of the smoke. *SMS Lützow* torpedoed *Defence*, which then came under fire from *SMSs Grosser Kurfürst, Markgraf, Kronprinz* and *Kaiser*. Within a few short minutes a concentrated fire was raining down on *Defence*. After taking a number of hits, she simply blew up. After spending so many months chasing German ships, then waiting patiently in port for "Der Tag", Abercrombie and his colleagues on *Defence* had lasted a matter of minutes in combat. A stunned officer on board a nearby ship, the *Obedient,* wrote that after the explosion "we could see no sign of a ship at all – *Defence* had gone."

A sense of the confusion of the battle, as well as the shock of *Defence's* demise, can be gathered from this account by Commander George Von Hase, Chief Gunnery Officer on the German battleship *Derfflinger*:

"At 8.15pm 31 May 1916 we received a heavy fire. Lieutenant Commander Hausser, who had been firing at a torpedo boat with our secondary battery, asked me, 'Sir, is this cruiser with the four funnels a German or an English cruiser?' I directed my periscope at the ship and examined it. In the grey light the colour of the German and the English ships looked almost exactly the same. The cruiser was not at all far from us. She had four funnels and two masts exactly like our Rostock who was with us. 'It is certainly English,' exclaimed Lieutenant Commander Hausser; 'May I fire?' 'Yes - fire away!' I said. I became convinced that it was a large English ship. The secondary guns were aimed at the new target and Hausser commanded, '69 hundred!' At the moment in which he was about to order 'Fire!' something horrible, something terrific happened. The English ship which I meanwhile supposed to be an old English battle cruiser, broke asunder and there was an enormous explosion. Black smoke and pieces of the ship whirled upward, and flame swept through the entire ship, which then disappeared before our eyes beneath the water. Nothing was left to indicate the spot where a moment before a proud ship had been fighting, except an enormous cloud of smoke. According to my opinion, the ship was destroyed by the fire of the ship just ahead of us – the *Lutzow*, the flagship of Admiral Hipper.

The whole thing lasted only a few seconds and then we engaged with a new target. The destroyed ship was the *Defence*, one of the older armoured cruisers of the same type as the *Black Prince* which was sunk by gunfire the following night. She displaced 14, 800 tons, was armed with six 23.4 centimetre and ten 15.2 centimetre guns and had a crew of 700 men. Of the crew not a single soul was rescued. The ship was blown into atoms and every living soul was destroyed by the explosion. I shall never forget the sight I saw through my periscope in all its gruesomeness."

It should be noted that Von Hase underestimated the number of men on board the *Defence*. Abercrombie was one of 903 men, all killed in that instant. The losses at Jutland were notable in that when ships were lost, whole crews went with them. Of the 1,286 men on board the *Queen Mary*, all but 20 were killed. A major reason for this lies with the fact that the British gun turrets on their ships proved susceptible to direct hits because the emphasis in training on rapid fire techniques meant that cordite was stored in the open. There were several examples of catastrophic flash explosions of British ships, and the *Defence* was a clear example of this.

At the time, it was believed that *Defence* had been atomised by the explosion, but the wreck was discovered in 2001 by a diving team and found to be largely intact, although the hull appears to have been melted by the heat of the flash. Abercrombie's ship lies in around 45m of water and the wreck was given protected status in 2006 under the Protection of Military Remains Act 1986.

Admiral of the Fleet Lord Fisher described Arbuthnot's actions, and by extension the demise of the *Defence* as "a glorious but not a justifiable death". What the families made of such a conclusion is difficult to imagine. There is no record of what Cecily Abercrombie thought. Her experience of life with her husband was rather like that of the Hampshire players and supporters, all too brief.

Hesketh Hesketh-Pritchard

In February of 1914 there was a gathering of Edwardian England's most famous explorers at Prae Wood, near St Albans, the home of Lady Elizabeth Grimston. Her husband was Hesketh Vernon Hesketh-Prichard, an explorer, adventurer, big-game hunter and a Hampshire cricketer from 1900 till 1913. He had invited such figures as Apsley Cherry-Garrard, one of the survivors of the recent ill-fated Scott expedition, to the house to meet his circle of friends. Indeed, the shadow of Scott's death must have loomed large, and Hesketh-Prichard's gathering must have been keen to hear a first-hand account. Perhaps Scott's famous line – "Englishmen can endure hardships, help one another, and meet death with as great a fortitude as ever in the past" – would have been a source of some pride to his dinner guests. Hesketh-Prichard's generation was a product of the Empire. He had been born in Uttar Pradesh in India, and had never known his father.

49

Hesketh Brodrick Pritchard died six weeks before his son's birth. On an expedition in Afghanistan, he had drunk from a stream at the side of the road, only to turn the next corner up the valley to see the same stream running through a filthy farmyard. At camp that night he told his companions, "I drank my death today". Typhoid claimed him just a few days later. He had been married just nine months. His son became the man of the house from day one.

Scott's sacrifice, as brave as it was ultimately pointless, struck a chord with men like Hesketh-Prichard, who had already explored the trackless wastes of Labrador and travelled amongst the exotic peoples of Haiti and Patagonia. When pressed for a judgement on Scott, Cherry-Garrard may have used a line from his book, *The Worst Journey in the World,* when he said, "We were as wise as anyone can be before the event." Sitting in the dining room of the house at Prae Wood, it's doubtful that anyone seriously imagined that another, far greater event was on the horizon, an event demanding greater sacrifices, and no less fortitude, than that shown by Scott and his party. A hundred years later, some people also wonder if, like Scott's expedition, this sacrifice was pointless too.

Hesketh-Pritchard had more immediate concerns in the winter of 1914. He was taking part in a cricket tour of Egypt, although, now in his late thirties, his once revered fast bowling was losing its bite. He was a popular cricketer, his easy style and sharp sense of humour making him an ideal colleague and tourist. "Hex", as he was known by friends and family, had taken to the game as a schoolboy. After seeing a cricket match for the first time at Jersey College, he was swept away with a boyish enthusiasm for the game. Like many before and since, he began to practise his bowling in the back garden. The family house – "Almorah" – is now a hotel, an idyllic spot, with views of the cliffs near St Helier.

In 1887 he arrived at Fettes College, Edinburgh, more recently famous (or, in some quarters, infamous) as the alma mater of Prime Minister Tony Blair. Hex had won a scholarship, but soon his love of cricket was noted by his tutor as having a negative impact on his academic work. At one point he was banned from playing at all as a punishment. Like many schoolchildren Hex struggled to come to terms with the attitude of the institution towards their sporty charges. By the time he was 17 years of age, Hex had already been chosen to play in a representative match against the touring South African side, but still felt alienated by the pressure he was being put under to keep his academic standards high. His decision to leave school a year early was an indication of the young man's strength of mind. According to the school magazine, Fettes was losing a bowler that was as good as anyone at the school could remember.

Hex moved to Sussex to pursue a legal career, and played club cricket for Horsham. He was also a keen writer, and collaborated with his mother on a number of projects. The loss of his father in Afghanistan meant that mother and son were very close. They were able to establish a reputation under the pen names of "E. and H. Heron", which brought Hex to the attention of London literary society. Upon gathering that Hex was also a fast bowler of some quality, Sir Arthur Conan-Doyle recruited him for his Allahakbarries touring side. The creator of Sherlock Holmes was a cricketing nut, and a friend of the greatest cricketing figure of the time – indeed, some might say of all time – W.G. Grace. For all Conan-Doyle's achievements, he treasured the fact that his only first class cricket wicket was that of the "Good Doctor". The fact that a fatigued W.G. had skied a rank long hop after scoring a century was irrelevant, as it would be to any star struck bowler. For Hex, the contact with both these men helped him on his way. Conan-Doyle put him in touch with the likes of Arthur Pearson, the owner of the Daily Express, which resulted in some writing work. W.G. Grace recruited him to play cricket for London County. From 1902 to 1904, Hex turned out for this newly formed side when his other commitments allowed.

One of those commitments was Hampshire C.C., who had won the race for his signature in 1900. An invitation from Sussex via his club at Horsham had failed to reach its intended recipient, so Hampshire became his county from 1900 to 1913. In that time he bowled well over 1,700 overs, taking 233 wickets at an average of 23.45. Neville Cardus, writing about

Hesketh-Pritchard in the *Manchester Guardian*, felt that his was an exceptional talent. As a tall, athletic man, he was able to make a good length ball climb off the most benign surface. Cardus also noted that he had the good sense to change his style to adapt to conditions. On a rain affected wicket, Hesketh-Pritchard would throttle back on the pace and bowl off cutters. He was a thinking cricketer – not something that out and out fast bowlers are accused of too often. On his day, however, he was a real destructive force, taking five wickets in an innings on fifteen occasions for Hampshire. On his county debut, he had caused a stir by clean bowling the highly regarded Somerset batsman L.C.H. Palairet on his way to a three wicket haul. In his first full season, 1902, he repeated the feat, removing the legendary C.B. Fry in a match against Sussex. The cricketing public would have noted his skittling of seven Derbyshire batsmen for 47 runs on what was described in a press review as a "perfect Southampton wicket".

His cricketing reputation was growing, and a healthy haul of 45 wickets in the 1903 season was rewarded by selection for the prestigious Gentlemen v Players match at Lords. He failed to reproduce his excellent county form at cricket's HQ – perhaps not surprisingly, as the young debutante was asked to bowl uphill into a stiff breeze. Nevertheless, he was selected to play for the M.C.C. in 1904, causing a sensation by dismissing all five top-order Kent batsmen without conceding a run. That season saw Hex heading the Hampshire averages, taking 62 wickets at an average of 24. Back at Lord's, in his third successive appearance in the Gentlemen v Players match, it was his batting that drew the plaudits. He helped put on 51 for the last wicket in the first innings and then helped A.O. Jones to accumulate the winning runs in the second innings. The opposition fielders crowded round him, confident of gaining the last wicket to win the match, but Hex played soundly in defence to frustrate them. "I have witnessed many a century that was not worth half as much," purred one correspondent. On another occasion he decided to block out against the formidable touring Australian side in their match against Hampshire, and the report on the game describes Hex roaring with laughter when he edged a four through the slips. The Australians must have thought it was hilarious.

This defensive thinking was very much out of character, as Hex had the reputation of being a hard hitter of a cricket ball. His first class career batting average of just under 7.5 would suggest that he was a hit and miss tailender, with perhaps a tendency towards the latter. *The Star*'s cricket correspondent described his batting style as "like a child scooping out sand with a spade." While this is hardly flattering, it may go some way towards explaining that average. Like many specialist bowlers, he enjoyed batting, and his willingness to chance his arm sometimes saw him promoted into the middle order. He was good box office for the crowds.

In the following year, his busy schedule only allowed him time to play five county matches, although he managed to take 39 wickets at an average of just over 24. Unluckily for the poor Derbyshire batsmen, he was available for their fixture, and took a career best 8 wickets for just 32 runs in the second innings to win the game. The opposition captain on the day, A.E. Lawton, had this to say about his county's bête noir:
"When he bowls very fast, with a perfect length, pitches the ball on the leg stump and knocks the off out of the ground, there is nothing for it but to bow politely and depart..."

In 1907 Hex was given the honour of captaining the M.C.C. on an overseas tour to the United States. Although opponents such as The Gentlemen of Philadelphia were not overly taxing as opponents, the M.C.C. selectors sent Hex out with a squad brim-full of talent. The side included his erstwhile Hampshire colleague and hunting partner, E.G. Wynyard, as well as a future England captain, J.W.H.T. Douglas. It was an exercise in cricketing diplomacy, as much as anything else, and Hex was clearly chosen for the role because of his status within the game. He was into his thirties, and his body would have been complaining about the stresses and strains of fast bowling, particularly when bearing in mind that he was not a full time cricketer.

Right from the start of his career, Hex showed himself to be a man of many talents. Indeed, the very use of the word "career" seems inaccurate. As a "gentleman player" Hex would play when he could. Occasionally,

cricket would take a backseat while he pursued his other great love –
travel. Initially he travelled to accumulate material for his writing projects.
His optician inadvertently fed this bug by telling him that a recurring eye
condition might be helped with prolonged exposure to sea air. Hex took
this as an excuse to sail across the Atlantic to Panama. The 4,500 mile
journey gave him more material for his short stories and travel pieces for
magazines such as the *Pall Mall*. He was very much in demand. C.B. Fry,
who ran his own magazine and who became a Hampshire team mate,
asked him to write something:
"Is there any chance of you being persuaded to write me a story or two?
2,500 – 3,000 word 'storiettes'? These would have the advantage of not
interfering with your big efforts, and would be, in effect, extras – leg byes
as compared with your high on-drives..."

As we have already seen, Hex's "high on-drives" were only occasionally
successful. The diplomatic Fry would hardly use the term "slog over cow
corner". What is interesting to note here from a modern perspective is that
Hex's "big efforts" are nothing to do with his first class cricketing exploits.
The "efforts" in question were his expeditions to such out of the way places
as Haiti and Patagonia, and the writing that these trips engendered. Books
such as *In Trackless Labrador*, published in 1911, fed the public's thirst for
adventure, and Hex's first-hand accounts proved extremely popular.
Editors and readers alike enjoyed his account of journeys to the
unpromising interior of Labrador, where Hex and his companion cross
mosquito plagued wastes, hunt bears, consume squirrel soup and sack
Eskimo guides who dare to ask for more money. In 1902, Arthur Pearson of
the *Daily Express* had contracted him to hunt down the legendary giant
sloth, a journey that resulted in a book called *Through the Heart of
Patagonia*. Hex had, from a young age, enjoyed shooting, and he was
generally recognised to be one of the finest shots in the country. He even
went hunting on his honeymoon, persuading his young wife that the
perfect way to celebrate their wedding was to hunt seals off the coast of
Norway.

When war was declared Hex felt sure that he could make his own contribution, but his age (37) meant that he was rejected for commissions with the Black Watch and the Guards. He was eventually able to secure a post as an Assistant Press Officer with the War Office, tasked with accompanying journalists out to the Western Front. Given Lord Kitchener's legendary distrust of Fleet Street, and Hex's own frustration at not being in the thick of things, it is not surprising that from the moment he set foot in France in February 1915 he was eager to move on.

By this time, it was clear that the war was going to be a long drawn out affair. It had failed to be over by Christmas, and the establishment of a line of trenches from the North Sea to the Swiss border was ominous. He witnessed the effects of one of the first gas attacks, and was profoundly shocked by this development. He was also shocked to see that German snipers were so clearly superior to their Allied opponents. British units were losing five men a day on average, with one battalion suffering eighteen casualties being the worst example. With his experience as a hunter and expert rifleman, Hex could see that these losses were to large degree avoidable. Spurred on by seeing young men with terrible head wounds being ferried away from the frontline trenches, he began a one man campaign to redress matters. His hunting instincts told him that Allied tactics were all wrong. After the war, he wrote up an account of this campaign in a book – *Sniping in France*. It detailed his initial observations, and described the unusual path his military career took. The man who was initially rejected for a commission became a highly prized expert whose intelligence and skills saved many lives, and eventually turned the tables on the German snipers.

One of Hex's first observations was that approximately 80% of British sniping rifles were "quite useless", as the telescopic sights were not calibrated correctly. The sights were handed out as trench stores, and the "sniper" often had little idea how to use the equipment. By comparison, the Germans had over 20,000 good quality telescopic sights fitted to rifles, used by men who had been trained for the purpose. Hex began to take his own rifle with him in his forays into the trenches, and would spend time adjusting sights and talking to troops. He also began to ask his hunting friends back home to send their own rifles out to France. He had found his calling. As he notes in *Sniping in France*, it "was really neither more nor less than a very high class form of big game shooting."

It was also plain to the hunter that the high attrition rate of Allied snipers, as well as the effectiveness of the opposition, was due to a poor appreciation of the importance of concealment. A lack of basic training in this crucial element of the sniper's art was losing lives. The superior German snipers were more adept at hiding out in No Man's Land, and the casualties they were inflicting were having a real effect on morale. Hex explained all this to Lieutenant-Colonel A.G. Stuart, who proved a valuable ally. He set up a meeting with Sir Charles Munro, Commander of the Third Army, and Hex was seconded as their "sniping expert". Now that he had an official function, he could set about the task of training the men, and improving their equipment. John Buchan, the author of *The Thirty-Nine Steps* who was working as a war correspondent with *The Times*, proved to be another useful ally.

Before he began his new job, Hex had some home leave. Before crossing the channel, however, he rummaged through some abandoned German trenches at Neuve-Chappelle and salvaged some German metal sniper shields. He spent much of his time on leave firing different calibre bullets at the shields, noting that the standard British sniping ammunition was effectively useless. Again, he was able to effect change by using his initiative. This restlessness would occasionally raise hackles, but Hex realised the need to press ahead if he was to save lives. In *Sniping in France* he tells the story of how he overheard one sceptical officer at the front: "'Who is this Blighter who is coming?' And then someone gave my name. Then a voice said: 'Plays cricket, doesn't he?'"

His cricketing fame was getting his foot in the door again. Soon, however, his work was paying off, and the cynics were won over. Hex devised some interesting methods, and they were a great success. One can only imagine the reaction when he ordered papier mâché heads to be made at a theatrical workshop in Amiens, but when these realistic models were raised above the parapet of the trench, the subsequent bullet wound allowed the Allied troops to calculate the position of the concealed German sniper. The imagination and level of detail that Hex put into his work were notable. When the Germans began to realise that these heads were fake, Hex made them appear more realistic by putting cigarettes in their mouths that were then "smoked" through a rubber tube to create a tempting tell-tale cloud just above the parapet.

From the very start of the war, the Allied had made it more difficult for themselves in terms of concealment by building these parapets in an orderly, uniform manner. The Germans varied their shapes, and used different coloured sandbags to help their snipers make themselves less obvious. Hex devised "drainpipe" loopholes, set at different angles to the opposition line, to make it difficult to return fire. He also invented sniping shields with a sliding second metal loophole a few inches behind the front plate, which cut the chances of a successful opposing sniper making a "kill" – it was calculated that to get through both loopholes was twenty times less likely. Even so, Hex coached his charges to open these loopholes with great care, preferably never with the sun shining through them to give away the position. Gradually, Hex noted, these changes began to alter the balance of power in No Man's Land. The ability of the Allied snipers, now trained at Sniping Schools set up under his guidance at Steenbeque and Linghem, was now, in Hex's words, making it "very hot" for the German snipers, and for their forward artillery "spotters". The use of heavier calibre bullets by Allied snipers was also a major weapon against machine gunners. Allied snipers were able to fire at the machine guns themselves, putting them out of action, rather than the more difficult task of trying to hit the men behind the metal plate. In a war that was defined by artillery and machine guns, Hex's work was rightly praised.

All of this came at considerable personal cost, however. He had suffered a gas attack while in the front line, and doctors wondered if he was suffering from sepsis as a result of this incident when he was withdrawn from France in the spring of 1918. There is no doubt that he had worked himself into the ground, too, spurred on by witnessing the horrific results of head wounds from German sniping "kills". Hex battled through a series of operations in the next four years. The symptoms of extreme fatigue and anxiety, coupled with recurring heart and digestion problems, was put down to blood poisoning, although it may well be that he was suffering from malaria picked up on his pre-war travels. Through it all, he was writing up his wartime experiences in *Sniping in France*, and saw one of the stories he had written with his mother taken up by a Hollywood cinema. By the time *Don Q, Son of Zorro* was released in 1925, Hex was dead.

In his last few months, his close friend Eric Parker was in constant touch, visiting him at his home near St Albans. Parker wrote a brief life which he published in 1924. In it he describes the last few conversations with Hex, as he was finishing *Sniping in France*. His friend would excitedly retell his stories from France, but gradually "his eagerness became feverish, his crowded memories, the things he had seen and the things he would not talk about, seemed to me too much for him – he had borne too much. There were things, I knew, about which he did not wish to talk; I wondered whether there were things of which he tried not to think."

In January 1913 a wooden cross was erected by the surviving members of Scott's Antarctic party at Observation Hill on Ross Island. The names of those lost on the expedition are inscribed there, along with a quote from Tennyson's epic poem to the Victorian spirit, *Ulysses* – "To strive, to seek, to find, and not to yield." These words would have struck a chord with Hesketh-Prichard, whose adventurous spirit led him on a series of quests. He was a successful writer and journalist. His fast bowling made him a feared opponent, and a much loved team mate. But of all his qualities, it was his willingness to "strive", the unwillingness to "yield" that turned out to be the defining feature of his life. It was this bloody mindedness that made him overcome the obstacles that were put in his way during the war, and led to his greatest achievement. His good friend George Gray pointed out that before Hex began his work, a single battalion on the Western Front would lose an average of five men a week to enemy snipers. With Hex's methods established, only 44 deaths were reported over a period of three months by sixty battalions. By Gray's calculations, Hex had saved 3,500 lives during the First World War. How many descendants of those men there are living a century later is difficult to say. A common assumption is that each person has 500 descendants after a hundred years, which would equate to 1,750,000 people having Hesketh Vernon Hesketh-Pritchard to thank for their very existence. Not a bad legacy.

The Hon. Lionel H. Tennyson

Coping with rain delays has always been one of the bugbears of the cricket fan. At the Ageas Bowl, the frustrated supporter could do worse than stroll up to the mezzanine level of the Atrium building, where there is an impressive collection of cricketing memorabilia and photographs. In a glass case on one of the walls is an old bat. The modern cricketer notes the dark stain of the wood and the lack of logos, but it appears at first sight to be pretty unremarkable. The kind of antique piece of sporting equipment you might stumble over in a loft. But this bat tells a remarkable story of its own, and its owner was arguably the most important figure in Hampshire cricket in the first half of the twentieth century. The bat belonged to the Honourable Lionel Hallam Tennyson, the county captain from 1919 till 1933. He was also, for one brief spell, the captain of England.

During the Ashes summer of 1921, the England team was, by general consensus, a poor match for Warwick Armstrong's rampaging Australian side. After two thumping Australian victories at Trent Bridge and Lord's, the England selectors followed the advice of one of the game's greats, C.B. Fry, who suggested that his young Hampshire captain might just provide the spark the national team required. Tennyson was renowned as an aggressive batsman who enjoyed facing the pacemen on the County circuit. In Jack Gregory and Ted MacDonald the touring side had two of the greatest exponents of fast bowling the world had ever seen.

So it was that the scene was set – Tennyson was chosen to take the fight to the Australians. He looked down and out before facing a ball, however, having suffered a serious hand injury while fielding in the Australian first innings at Headingley. The crowd wondered if they would see the new captain bat at all. At seven wickets down in the England innings, Tennyson strode down the steps and walked out onto the grass. His injured hand was protected by a wire cage, and he was clutching the bat in his "good" hand. There was a collective gasp as the spectators realised that Tennyson was going out to face the most feared bowling attack in the world one handed. Throughout his career, he established a reputation for unflinching bravery in the face of the quicker bowlers. Indeed, he seemed to positively thrive on the challenge. What occurred in the next hour and twenty minutes at Leeds went some way towards cementing that reputation, as Tennyson took the Australian bowlers on. He scored 63 runs, clipping the ball to the boundary on ten occasions, in an inspirational display of skill and courage. It was one of those unique "I was there" moments for the

Yorkshire faithful. He went on to score 36 in the second innings, but he could not stop another Australian victory. Despite the fact that they had won the series, Tennyson's heroics had galvanised his team, and put some pride into the hearts of their long suffering supporters. His side fought out two respectable draws in the final two tests of the series. In what, even now, feels like a mindless piece of selectorial vandalism, Tennyson was dropped in the wake of the series, and never played for England again. The bat in its glass case at the Ageas Bowl gives us a snapshot into the career of one of Hampshire's most gifted, and occasionally most controversial, players.

As the grandson of the Poet Laureate, he was able to claim Hampshire residency due to the family home on the Isle of Wight, Farringford. In one of his autobiographical books, *Sticky Wickets*, Tennyson gives the reader an insight into how constrained he felt by life in the shadow of the great poet of Victorian England. His relationship with his father, the poet's adoring son, was difficult as a result.

"It was an atmosphere of veneration, indeed, that was almost religious, and anything that tended even in the slightest degree to impair it he visited with the severest disfavour. His observations frequently began with the words 'My father said' or 'My father thought'. In fact, he seemed to refer all questions of importance to that past oracle, so mighty in its own day, and may be said never to have wholly emerged from the Victorian age."

Lionel Tennyson lived a life largely free of the shackles of the Victorian Age. In his excellent biography of the Hampshire captain Alan Edwards suggests that he escaped these shackles by going back, rather than forwards, in time. Edwards describes him as a "Regency Buck", as far away from his age as we are from him today.

Interestingly, *The Bookman*'s review of his first autobiography *From Verse to Worse* in 1933 detected a lack of confidence in the man – "we feel throughout that the author is labouring under an unnecessary but perfectly understandable inferiority complex." This observation would be something that his friends and acquaintances over the years would have simply laughed out of court. It may have been that his cricketing exploits allowed him to break the shackles that had always attached his father to the Victorian Age. It is interesting to note that when he puts his cricket bat down, however, and begins to write, the doubts do crowd in.

"There always seemed an atmosphere about Farringford which it was extremely difficult to live up to. Perhaps no one without a similar experience could understand exactly what I mean."

Perhaps Tennyson relished playing the role of the naughty boy? He would not be the first, or the last, first class cricketer to do so. Some sound recorders turned up at Farringdon towards the end of the poet laureate's life in order to preserve the great man's voice for posterity. Young Lionel, as respectful as ever, was accused of sabotaging the recordings by making rude noises in the background.

The family spent some time in Australia, where his father worked as a diplomat, and his son learned to play cricket on hard fast surfaces. Throughout his career he relished the ball coming onto the bat, and much of this can be ascribed to his Australian upbringing. When he went to boarding school back in England, he struggled to make any sort of sustained impact with the bat. He found it difficult to adjust to the seam movement and sluggish pace of early season English pitches, and he was principally employed as a bowler during his time at Eton. He was quick but inconsistent – later in his career a correspondent described him as "a bowler of the fast and furious type that is generally beloved of real batsman." It was the same story when he tried to make a breakthrough in University cricket when he attended Trinity College, Cambridge.

By this time his conservatively minded father had become increasingly nervous about his son's high octane lifestyle. When Lionel left Cambridge, he joined the Coldstream Guards, whose ranks were filled with the sons of the well heeled. Lionel's father was against the move, and his fears proved to be well founded. Lionel was drawn into the social maelstrom that was London society, and was sinking into debt. In *Sticky Wickets* he gives us a unique insight into the thinking of the obsessive gambler. When he realises that he is in a hole, he decides to keep digging. He describes his response to mounting debt - a little more judicious betting. The fall, when it came, was precipitous. Tennyson lost £12,000 in a week at race meetings, and the only way of saving face was to leave the Guards. He joined the Rifle Brigade.

Perhaps sobered by this personal financial crisis, he took his cricket more seriously. Tennyson started to be noticed at Army level for his clean hitting. It may be that he had finally adapted to English pitches. He averaged over 60 in the 1913 season, and was rewarded with an invitation to play for the MCC against Oxford University. He made a promising 28 in the first innings, then exploded into form with a century in the second innings of his first first-class cricket match. Now he was on the national cricketing radar. The fact that he listed the Tennyson family house at Farringford, on the Isle of Wight, as his principal residence meant that Hampshire seized the opportunity to sign him up, and he made his Hampshire debut against Worcestershire on 21st July, 1913.

His debut performance was pure Tennyson – 28 runs in twenty balls, with 24 of those runs coming in boundaries. Unsurprisingly, the crowd took to him straight away. Throughout his career, he would be the sort of batsman who would empty the bars.

Hampshire's next game was at Leyton, where their bowlers were flayed by the Essex batsmen for a huge score of 507. Tennyson contributed a bright and breezy 38 to the Hampshire reply, but his team was still 317 runs behind when they began their second innings. Shortly afterwards, three top-order Hampshire batsmen were back in the pavilion with Essex still well over 300 runs ahead. So it was that the young Rifle Brigade officer strode to the wicket toward the end of the second day. Essex players and fans could afford to be in an indulgent mood, with the game seemingly in the bag. An hour and a half later, however, Tennyson was closing in on a chanceless century, and he had turned the tide of the match. His innings contained 17 boundaries, and his final score of 116 was out of a Hampshire total at that stage of 186. The quality of the innings was overshadowed by the stunning seventh wicket partnership of 325 between George Brown and Cecil Abercrombie, a record breaking performance that still lives on in the Hampshire record books, but it was Tennyson's controlled hitting that did so much to change the course of the game.

Tennyson's golden summer continued at Trent Bridge, where he again teamed up with E.M. Sprot to produce 132 runs in only an hour. Tennyson scored 111, an innings liberally sprinkled with sixteen boundaries. In the next match on the road at Harrogate, he took on the famed Yorkshire bowling attack only to fall four runs short of another century. It would have been his fourth century in the first five matches of his first class career.

In between matches for Hampshire, he continued his good form in Army cricket. Tennyson was living life to the maximum, still attending functions in London in the evenings, then somehow able to see the ball well enough to send it to the boundary the next day. A fellow officer recalled one occasion when he returned from a successful week with Hampshire only to be bowled first ball in a game for the battalion. It was said that the reason for the dismissal was that he had got to bed far too early the previous evening.

Army duties removed him from the team sheet for much of August. Just as he was in the form of his life, professional duties called him away, a typical state of affairs for the amateur game. It is difficult to say how much of a frustration this was, as it was considered to be the way of the world at the time. Modern day county cricket fans are often frustrated by their favourite players being declared unavailable because of national selection, but again, deep down, they recognise that local interests must of necessity play second fiddle to the priorities of the national side. One suspects that the attitude towards servicemen such as Tennyson, Johnston and Abercrombie being called away was something akin to this sense of good natured resignation. A shrug of the shoulders, a quiet comment about wishing they could see an innings from a Tennyson or a Greenidge or a Gower, and then they would settle down to their day's cricket.

Tennyson returned to the fray in late August, smashing fourteen boundaries in an innings of 83 against Gloucestershire. He found the perfect partner in Philip Mead. So often the man once called "The Rock of Ages" would play the anchor role for Hampshire, and the blend of his seemingly impregnable defence and Lionel Tennyson's free flowing style would have broken West Country hearts. Tennyson rubbed salt in their wounds with an attacking 46 in the second innings, again in collaboration with Mead, who went on to put the game well beyond their reach with a mammoth score of 171. At the end of his remarkable first season, Tennyson stood second to Mead in the Hampshire batting averages, and fifth in the entire country. *Wisden* recognised the extent of his contribution by naming him as one of their top "Five Cricketers of the Year". "Rarely indeed has a player quite new to first class matches done so much," said the editor. Attacking batsmen always arouse a degree of suspicion in some quarters, so *Wisden* did leave the reader with an ambivalent note on Tennyson's potential – "he may or may not have the qualities that make for permanent success." The fact remains, however, that Tennyson's debut season was something quite extraordinary, the flowering of a talented player who had struggled to find his feet at school and university cricket.

All this made him difficult to overlook for an MCC tour to South Africa in October of 1913, which his army masters were happy to sign off. The young batsman rubbed shoulders with some of the biggest names in the game – Jack Hobbs, Frank Woolley and Wilfred Rhodes were all on board the *SS Saxon* as it set sail. As confident a social animal as Tennyson was, he would have been happy to see the familiar face of Philip Mead in the squad. Tennyson struggled to make an impact in the four match series, despite an early half century. Just three months into his first class career, he found it difficult to adjust to the vagaries of batting on matted wickets, where the movement off the pitch made forcing shots early in your innings a risky proposition.

He averaged only 20 on tour. Unsurprisingly, he very much enjoyed the social aspect of touring. He was, throughout his life, an enthusiastic traveller, as detailed in his autobiographical works – *From Verse to Worse* and *Sticky Wickets*. Like many children of the Victorian Empire, he relished the opportunity to see the world. Cricket, of course, was the quintessential Imperial export, and English sides would be welcomed all over the globe. Touring teams were entertained lavishly – not something that Lionel Tennyson was going to object to. He would have gained a great deal from the experience as a cricketer, and would have had his ambitions stirred by his selection in such a highly rated side.

By the time he returned to English shores, however, it was April 1914, and the world was only a few weeks from catastrophe. Tennyson's cricketing aspirations were initially put on hold by the peace time Army necessities of training. His commanding officer made it clear that he would have to be away for the early part of the 1914 season, as he had already lost a good deal of "professional" time to cricket. After the euphoria of his first season, this must have been difficult to take. When he was allowed to play in 1914, he was inevitably out of form. His army training was due to wind down at the end of July, and he was looking forward to rejoining Hampshire for a run of matches. He played in some invitational matches in an effort to regain his touch, and was selected to play against Essex at Leyton. The scene was set for a triumphal return to the ground where he had announced his arrival on the first class scene just a year earlier. On the eve of the match, however, he was at his London flat when he heard the news that war had been declared. Tennyson had to return to barracks in Colchester. Little did he or his Hampshire fans know that he would not play for the County again for five long years.

The 1st Battalion Rifle Brigade, his unit, had already left for France, and Tennyson was to follow with a detachment of riflemen as soon as they were ready. He sailed from Southampton to Le Havre on the 23rd of August, and joined the battalion near Coulommiers. It must have been a strange mix of emotions at work on the young officer at that point. Perhaps he felt the rush of adrenalin that he would recognise as being something akin to facing an opening bowler. But he would be quick to realise that this was no game. The battalion had lost a significant number of men at Ligny, on the Retreat from Mons, and seeing the gaps in the ranks would have been a sobering moment.

To the north of Coulommiers, along the River Marne, the Allies were fighting back, and Tennyson had arrived in time for the tide to turn. Hampshire cricket fans would probably say that this was a good thing, as Tennyson was only likely to be successful when he was on the offensive. He was taking part in what became known as "The Miracle of the Marne", when the retreating B.E.F. joined the French counter attack and stopped what looked like an inevitable German victory. Gallieni, the French commander in charge of the defence of Paris, requisitioned taxis in the capital city, and thousands of French troops were ferried to the Marne, where they were thrown forward in an attack against the right flank of the advancing Germans. It was one of the key moments of the war. The historian Basil Liddell-Hart went as far to say that "Germany lost the war when she lost this battle."

Tennyson's Rifle Brigade troops crossed the Marne at La Ferte. It was a move that he had reconnoitred himself, and he had bumped into another renowned son of the Isle of Wight, Jack Seely. An ex-Cabinet minister, Seely and his horse Warrior would have been well known to Tennyson, and both men were establishing their reputations as officers who led from the front. Tennyson had already had to dash across open ground in a hail of machine gun fire to deliver orders to a neighbouring contingent of Lancashire Fusiliers. The fighting around La Ferte was short lived but ferocious. Tennyson, however, found La Ferte to be undefended when his troops crossed on September 9th. Crucially, it was now the German army that was in reverse, heading back towards the next river crossing, the Aisne. It was the turn of Moltke and the German High command, based in Luxemburg, to feel depressed by events. Some historians have felt that the two Allied commanders, Joffre and Sir John French, were too slow to take advantage of this about turn. The glacial pace of their decision making frustrated officers on the ground at the time, too.

These early exchanges of the war had taught the Allies an important lesson – that the firepower of the modern army made well prepared defensive positions very difficult to overcome. Every hour that went by, the troops knew, would be another hour the Germans could spend on the next defensive line. The Rifle Brigade pressed on towards the Aisne, crossing the river at night time on September 13th. They walked in single file at five yard intervals along the bridge's remaining girder. For any German defenders alive to the move, it would have been like shooting toy ducks at a fun fair. Tennyson's unit pushed through the village of Bucy-le-Long, so far in advance of where high command expected them to be that they were targeted by British artillery.

At this stage in the campaign, however, it was the remorseless accuracy of the German guns that caused difficulties. Tennyson and his men found shelter in a cave, disturbing a local hermit in the process. The only option for infantry was to dig trenches. The ferocity of the German bombardments stopped the allied advance in its tracks. Tennyson's diary shows how shocking the effects of these carefully targeted bombardments could be. He describes one of his men, an N.C.O. called Walker, having his leg almost completely blown off. This brave man takes his own pocket knife to cut through the remaining section of bone as he is lying out in the field. The tone of the diary shows Tennyson's commitment to his men, and he is critical of his superiors. He reflects on an advance in the face of the German defensive positions late in the day on the 13th September – "this stupid advance did no good, and we were forced to retire about 300 yards again." It was becoming clear that the opening movements of both sides, measured in miles gained per day, was settling down into the more familiar view that modern readers have of World War I, where advances are measured in yards. The following morning, Tennyson's men are digging trenches for all they are worth.

As German fire intensified on September 14th, Tennyson made contact with some officers from the Seaforth Highlanders, one of whom was Colonel Evelyn Bradford. He had played cricket for Hampshire from 1895 till 1905. An all rounder, his fast bowling had created quite an impact when he first arrived on the count scene, most notably when he took eleven wickets in a match against Essex in 1896. Soon, however, there were whispers about the suspect nature of his action. Despite his highly impressive first class average of 16.40, he only played for the county on eight occasions. Now in his forty sixth year, Colonel Bradford gives the lie to the stereotype of the Great War officers all being safe behind the lines in comfortable French chateaus. Just after his conversation with Tennyson, he was killed by a German shell as he left the trench and is buried at the cemetery at Crouy-Vauxrot.

The Rifle Brigade's experiences in the next few weeks were typical of those of most British troops. The stress of being under fire in the day was compounded by the fact that many troops had to work through the night on the defences. A 250 meter section of trench would take approximately 2700 man hours to complete, and German gunners were not going to allow such activity in broad daylight. Both armies were exhausted by the campaigns they had fought in over August and September, but now they were being tested psychologically by trench warfare, a type of warfare that was to be the norm for the next four years.

As the hot summer of 1914 gave way to autumn, the armies moved northwards in an effort to outflank opposition trenches. In this "Race to the Sea", the Western Front became delineated by over 10,000 km of trenches. The Rifle Brigade joined this move northward, finding that the clay of Flanders was easier to dig than the chalk of Picardy. But with the onset of winter, it was becoming obvious that it was more difficult to maintain these trenches. Drainage was a major problem, with the combination of a high water table and the local clay's ability to hold water making life uncomfortable, at best. "Trench foot" became as significant as German artillery and snipers in terms of casualties lost from frontline duties.

Tennyson's unit was based near St Omer in October, and both sides continued to test out the opposition's territory as the trench lines moved closer to the Channel. It was crucial that the B.E.F. should not find itself to be outflanked. Tennyson took a detachment of men up the road into the town of Bailleul, and surprised some German troops there. He rounded up 68 prisoners and marched them back to Allied lines.

The Rifle Brigade moved eastwards to the Armentieres sector, where the manoeuvring quietened down once more, and the spade took over from the gun. At the end of October the Germans launched a major attack in his sector. The market town of Ypres, just a few miles to the north, had become the focal point for German efforts on the western front, the culmination of the Race to the Sea. The Rifle Brigade came under sustained fire as part of this campaign. Ypres was to be the scene of bitter fighting for the next four years, with three more campaigns from both sides attempting to gain control of this historic town and its infamous Salient. By 1918, it was little more than a pile of bricks.

Tennyson's men faced up to an assault lasting many days, defending trenches that had been shattered by German artillery fire and beating off waves of determined infantry attacks. They were relieved to see the King's Own Liverpool Regiment appear on the 9th November to relieve them of front line duty after nearly two weeks in the same position. Such was the pressure on the Allied line, however, that this was "relief" only in name. The Rifle Brigade men were digging trenches through the night, and Tennyson was struck in the leg by a German bullet. He tried to limp back to find cover, but fell headlong into a deep shell crater, causing major damage to muscles and ligaments in the process. It was, in the language of the trenches, a "Blighty One", and he was moved back behind the lines, then on to Boulogne. As he was sailing to Southampton he was amused to read that he had been killed in action. Fearing his mother's reaction, he sent a telegram to assuage her fears.

His injuries proved serious enough to keep him off duty until March of 1915, and even then he was only cleared for mounted duties. It was to be July before he would be back in France. Now, as a Staff captain, Tennyson was involved in the planning for the major offensive at Loos. On arriving in the area, Tennyson paid a visit to his old unit. He was aware that their numbers would have been depleted by the winter fighting, but he was shocked to discover the extent of the Rifle Brigade's losses. He met one of the soldiers who had crossed the Channel with him in September 1914, a Private who had been wounded in the arm. Like Tennyson, he had been eager to see the old faces on his return, only to discover that of the original one thousand men only six remained in the front line. Later in the year, at Christmas, Tennyson took part in a meal where several colleagues signed a menu card. He kept the card in a scrapbook, noting how many signatories did not survive the war. As a member of the officer class, Tennyson was acutely aware of the wastage rate. His own school, Eton, sent 5,560 officers to the Western Front, of whom 1,157 did not return.

When Haig was first asked to consider the plan to launch a full scale offensive in the Loos sector, he observed that the ground in the area was "unfavourable". Subsequent events proved that initial assessment to be correct. The Allies were to suffer nearly 60,000 casualties in the attack. For Tennyson, it was another sobering experience. In his Dairy he notes "the sights one saw today one will never forget. They were too horrible and dreadful..." Perhaps there is an element of guilt here. The failure at Loos was above all else a failure of planning, with reserves being kept too far from the support trenches to add weight when the battle got to a critical juncture. The subsequent political fallout lost Sir John French his job. Tennyson was probably happier to rejoin the troops in the trenches. He did so in October 1915 as second in command of the 10th Battalion and joined them in time to take part in what became known as the 2nd battle of Ypres. It was here that the Germans introduced the next Circle in what was becoming the Hell of trench warfare – poison gas.

Tennyson arrived home on leave in early 1916 at the end of his stint in Ypres to discover that his younger brother Harold had been killed when his ship *HMS Viking* struck a mine off Dunkirk. Grief stricken by the loss, he also worried about the effect on his ailing mother. In the funeral service at Freshwater, he would have been reflecting on how war losses were mounting, and now taking a toll on his own family.

Tennyson's unit was moved to the Somme in the summer of 1916, and he travelled up to the front line with the battle itself a few days old. His task was to try to restore some battered trenches, but his Diary shows the extent of his shock at the conditions.

"Never in my life had I been through anything like this. Dead faces were looking at one everywhere out of the mud, while the smell was too overpowering and awful for words..."

By the end of August, the 10th Battalion was in the front line, looking out of their trenches towards the German held village of Guillemont. Tennyson's unit was involved in furious hand to hand fighting in this sector and Guillemont was taken. He was wounded slightly, but fought on. Again, the newspapers reported him as killed in action, and again he sent a telegram to his parents. On the 28th September, however, he received a more serious wound to the mouth, and he was on the way back home again. Although the wound cleared up reasonable quickly, Tennyson was suffering from some shock. His mother found the strain of it all too much, following as it did on the death of Harold, and she became ill. She died on the 8th December, 1916. Tennyson had always been very close to his mother, perhaps a consequence of the uneasy relationship with his father, and he was devastated by her death. Typically, his autobiography strikes a carefree note as it describes his return to the trenches in France after the funeral at the start of 1917.

"I have never liked travelling light and so, though the amount of kit I arrived with may, in fact have aroused a certain amount of astonishment, I was quickly forgiven by my commanding officer as well as by everyone else, when they found out that it included, among other things, a case of champagne."

His group "lived like fighting cocks", he says, enjoying their time behind the lines. He describes a cricket match at Proven against the Guards Brigade which sounds as though it might be straight from the pages of a comic novel: cricketing fanatics spending hours preparing a wicket in a war zone, then losing their entire stock of balls in a pond which was unfortunately positioned in the middle of the ground.

All this must have seemed a million miles away from Tennyson's next engagement. His unit was involved in the attack on Pilckem Ridge in July 1917, in what became known as the battle of Passchendaele. It was, he said, "probably the foulest, grimmest and most costly battle..." The cemetery at Tyne Cot, the biggest Commonwealth War Grave site in the world, stands as testament to his words. A quarter of a million casualties was the price paid for what was also known (rather more depressingly) as the 3rd Battle of Ypres. Once again, however, Tennyson survived, only to be wounded again near Masnieres later in 1917. This attack, the Battle of Cambrai, was his last of the war.

Tennyson, now a Major, spent the rest of the war at the Machine Gun School at Grantham. He had fought in and survived all the major battles of this terrible war, and had been Mentioned in Despatches twice. He had lost numerous friends from his schooldays, adversaries from the cricket field and colleagues from the Rifle Brigade. In the last year of the war, he lost his other brother, Aubrey, killed in action on 22nd March, 1918. Perhaps his bitterness over the lack of any awards is a reflection of his bitterness towards the war itself.

Twenty years after leaving the Rifle Brigade, Tennyson served as a senior officer in charge of the air defence team at the airbase at Worthy Down. 806 Squadron flew Blackburn Skua fighter bombers for the Fleet Air Arm, patrolling the Channel, and defending the B.E.F. on the beaches of Dunkirk. In August of 1940, the base was attacked by a force of some 250 German planes, and perhaps Tennyson found cover in some of the slit trenches that had been dug around the perimeter of the runway. Quite what he made of being back in a trench is not recorded, but one can imagine that he would have puffed away at his signature pipe in an effort to give an outward show of calm insouciance for the benefit of his less experienced colleagues. Later in the war, Worthy Down was used as a staging post during the preparations for D-Day. Would the old warrior have been itching to get back across the Channel himself, one wonders. Bearing in mind that he had been wounded three times, and had lost two brothers as well as numerous friends, perhaps he watched younger men fly south in 1944 and felt as though he had "done his bit".

Tennyson was never decorated, despite his obvious bravery, and felt slighted by this fact. He saw some of his peers awarded medals, but perhaps he was always destined to remain on the fringes. He had made more than his fair share of enemies in the Establishment – there was an ugly scandal over his failed marriage, and the stigma of the gambling debts that had driven him out of the Guards into the more homely surroundings of the Rifle Brigade never really went away.

As a larger than life cricketer, beloved by the fans, a comparison can be made with Sir Ian Botham. Attack was always the best form of defence for both players, and they shared that certain X Factor that emptied bars even on the quietest days on the county circuit. Both men were made to feel as though they were outsiders by the cricketing powers-that-be, although obviously they started life in very different social circles. Cricket brought a state school lad like Botham into a position of real influence in the game, whereas Tennyson was, in a sense, born to wield power. Although some may feel that the stories of Tennyson's off-field exploits make Botham look like a choir boy, they both suffered their share of scandal, and both men were left feeling as though the Establishment was quick to judge them. Even though in Tennyson's day the newspapers were less interested in turning celebrities into front page fodder, His Lordship's marital and financial affairs were felt to be responsible for the fact that a man with such an exemplary military career should end the war without a medal. In 1981, the authorities were slow to back Botham's captaincy in the face of a rabid tabloid campaign, and quick to punish him for his admission that he had smoked cannabis in 1986. Botham was replaced as captain by that arch-Establishment figure, Mike Brearley. Tennyson was only given the England captaincy because the Lords choice for the job in 1921, the 49 year old C.B. Fry, told them that his Hampshire captain would be a better choice. Then, despite facing up to Warwick Armstrong's all conquering

Australian side and pulling his scratch side together to fight out two draws, Tennyson's captaincy was not renewed. Indeed, it was the end of his England career, seen by many as a shabby way to treat a man who had the courage to face the best fast bowlers of the age with a youth sized bat held in just one hand.

The most obvious heir to the Tennyson legacy at Hampshire was the captain of the County Champions of 1961, Colin Ingleby-Mackenzie. As captains, both men wore the mantle of leadership with a sense of natural ease, and committed to the idea that their teams should play attractive cricket. They batted in the same vein. They believed that the game should be enjoyed, on and off the field. Ingleby-MacKenzie once famously made his off-field expectations clear to his men by telling them to "be in bed by breakfast time." Lionel Tennyson would drink to that.

The boy who sabotaged his eminent grandfather's poetry recording back at Farringford always enjoyed taking the unconventional route. He could have tempered his batting when the team was in a tight corner, but he always stuck to his belief that he was more use to his team making runs than he might be trying to block his way out of a crisis. He could have also tempered his activities off the pitch – but, again, he was simply being true to his principles. A hundred years ago, famous sportsmen could live life freely. No one felt that what happened off the field of play was necessarily a case of public interest, and there were no newspaper proprietors who felt as though they should prove that that was the case. There was no social media to trip up the unwary sportsman. To establish the reputation that he did, meant that Lord Tennyson really had to go the extra mile.

On one celebrated occasion, Tennyson won the toss before a match against Middlesex, and then disappeared to take a long bath in order to regather his faculties after what had been a furious night of extra-curricular activity. When he emerged an hour or so later, he was appalled at the slow run rate, and decided to tell master batsman Phillip Mead as much. He did so by telegram via the local Post Office – "Too slow. Get out at once. Tennyson."

One might imagine that in an age when the professional cricketer was becoming a more common beast that old world amateurs such as Tennyson would create disharmony in a squad. Stunts such as sending telegrams out to the middle during an innings and late nights out at London clubs on match nights had dedicated pros such as Mead and Newman shaking their heads from time to time. His quixotic field placements occasionally riled his bowlers. But despite all these faults – perhaps even because of them, in some ways – Tennyson was universally loved by his team mates. It is significant that this dyed-in-the-wool amateur player should be one of the first captains to lead both professionals and amateurs out of the same gate on to the field of play. Once again, Tennyson was being true to his principles, and once again he upset the powers-that-be.

When asked for a comment on his Hampshire captain, the usually reserved Phillip Mead said, "He was a lovely man – just a big boy, really, and we would have followed him anywhere." In the years after the war to end all wars, his colleagues knew the value of a man who had survived the battles on the Marne, at Ypres, Loos, the Somme, Passchendaele and Cambrai. They knew that this was a man who had had to lead by example in the most terrifying of circumstances. Although he established his place in the Hampshire team by the prowess of his batting, he kept the captaincy for so long because he was a true leader, and his leadership skills were forged in the furnace of war.

Tennyson died in bed, cigar in hand, at his house at Bexhill on the 6th June, 1951. *The Observer*'s obituary on him ended thus – "He boomed through life like a great gush of wind. And many, far more than he could know, will miss the sound."

"Who shall return us our children?"

The country road that takes the traffic out of Peronne towards Albert affords the traveller some excellent views across the Somme valley to the south. The dramatic spur beyond the frontline village of Curlu is well worth the detour. But the tourist hoping to also catch some glimpse of the battlefield is in fact a few miles south of the ground which carries the litany of famous names on signposts that are etched into the history of the last century. Mametz, Fricourt, Pozieres, Bazentin all lie across the sweeping downland to the north. The committee that met after the war to name the various battles for posterity decided to name the great 1916 offensive The Battle of the Somme, although the river that runs through the battlefield is its tributary, the Ancre.

Beyond Curlu, the road crosses the old 1916 front line near Maricourt, and there is a sign for the village of Carnoy. The green Commonwealth War Graves Commission sign will lead the motorist down the hill to Carnoy Military cemetery. Established alongside a dressing station behind the lines, the cemetery contains 826 named casualties. One of the most frequently visited graves here is that of Captain Wilfred Percy Nevill, known as "Billie" to family and friends. A product of Dover College, where he captained the cricket team, "Billie" became famous when, as Commander of the 8th Battalion of the East Surrey Regiment, he presented his troops with four footballs that they were to kick across No Man's Land on July 1st 1916. It was not a new tactic – Nevill had heard of a soldier with the London Irish Rifles doing exactly this with his pals at the Battle of Loos the previous autumn. Nevill, recently attached to the Surreys having being commissioned in the Yorkshires, was perhaps aware that the huge preparatory bombardment had not removed the threat from German machine gunners on the ridge beyond Carnoy. Perhaps he was seeking a means of giving the men something else to think about, something that would keep them moving forwards. Nevill has attracted some cynicism in the years since the war, people accusing him of literally playing games with people's lives. For the Germans behind their machine guns, certainly, the whole stunt would have looked like madness. In Nevill's defence, however, it has to be said that the attack in the Carnoy sector of the front was one of the rare successes on the 1st of July. It also has to be said that Nevill led from the front. His body was found near the first German trench the next morning, near a couple of the footballs. They now reside in the regimental museum, and Nevill was buried within sight of his last and most famous action: his last game over at the age of 22.

The newspapers were desperate for some good news stories to come out of the disaster that was the first day of the Somme offensive. The casualty lists gave the lie to any reports that sought to paint too positive a picture, so Nevill's act of sporting derring-do was seized upon. The link between sport and war was something their readership could identify with, and Billie became a hero. "The Surreys played the game," crooned the *Daily Mail*. The popularity of Nevill's story, as evidenced by the continuing number of visitors to his graveside, shows that the story's mixture of bravery and eccentricity still has the power to attract an audience, so perhaps the *Mail* judged the public's mood right. There are other sportsmen, however, who prefer to see sport as a way of building bridges. They would focus instead on the football games in the snow between opposing sides during the unofficial Christmas truce of 1914.

The war over, the troopships brought the surviving men back to Southampton docks. The Hampshire team begins to re assemble – Mead, Newman, Livesey – the pros who were to inherit the game as the twentieth century wore on. These men were ever-present in the post war Hampshire county side. In a curious link from the old world to the new, Livesey became his captain's butler. Afterwards Tennyson used to joke that he couldn't remember if he hired him because he was his wicketkeeper, or that Livesey became his wicket keeper because he was his butler. Whatever the truth of the appointment, the dashing amateur batsman became the leader of a tight group of professional players. These men had been away for the whole of the war, sailing for India in October 1914. Although Indian first class continued throughout the war, army duties afforded the Hampshire exiles few opportunities to play at that level. There would, of course, have been inter unit matches, and presumably the

1ˢᵗ/5ᵗʰ Battalion would have been a feared opponent at the army grounds. No records survive, however.

Four Hampshire players – Newman, Livesey, Remnant and Greig - did appear in an England side for a match against a representative India XI at the Gymkhana Ground in Bombay in December 1915. Greig, who played periodically for Hampshire between 1901 and 1922, scored a mammoth 216 runs in the match. Newman and Livesey also appeared in the exotic sounding Maharaja of Cooch-Behar's XI at Eden Gardens, Calcutta in November 1917, where Newman's fast medium outswingers captured eight opposition wickets. This was listed as a first class game. Such players as Mead and Kennedy had to wait until the first week of June 1919 before making an entry into the first class world again, when they played in an MCC side against the Australian Imperial forces. Tennyson also played in that match, opening the first innings with a duck. Presumably he was attempting to hit the Australian quick bowler Jack Gregory out of St John's Wood. Philip Mead's thirst for runs had not been abated by his time away, however, and he scored over a hundred runs in the match. Hampshire fans would have thought that some things never change – that Tennyson was as unpredictable as Mead was dependable.

But of course things had changed. Lionel Tennyson had kept a scrapbook as well as a diary during the war, noting those who were close to him who had died. His old school friends from Eton had suffered huge losses – of the 5,660 Old Etonians who served, a staggering 1,157 died. The playing fields of his old school were credited with laying the foundations for victory at Waterloo. Now, a hundred years later, his school's community had paid a high price once more.

When the Foreign Secretary Sir Edward Grey said, "The lamps are going out all over Europe, we shall not see them lit again in our life-time." in the summer of 1914, he was of course speaking metaphorically. The First World War ended what is popularly known as county cricket's "Golden Age". Hampshire cricket suffered as much as any county team as the players and administrators bowed to what John Arlott called "the towering urgencies of war". The Hampshire fans would shake their heads and remember the flash of cricketing lightning that was Abercrombie's career. They had been deprived of the exciting prospect of a middle order composed of Tennyson and Abercrombie in full flow, at the peak of their powers, backed up by the relentless excellence of Jaques with the new ball. But deep down, they would also know that the scene before them – the immaculate cut of the grass, the sharp white lines, the evident bonhomie of the men playing out their collective boyhood dreams – represented an important part of the reason why all these people marched off to war. G.K. Chesterton once said, "The true soldier fights not because he hates what is in front of him, but because he loves what is behind him." Slowly, carefully, respectfully, cricket's lamps were being relit.

As memorials were erected in County pavilions in the years after the war, and the scars began to heal, people would reflect on the names etched there. They would think about their own families and neighbourhoods. Some would still be struggling under the shroud of grief as they remembered the one face amongst the hundreds that had waved to them from the deck of the troopship heading out of Southampton docks. For some families there was always going to be darkness. The sisters of the Yorkshire all rounder Major Booth lit a candle in his bedroom every night for the rest of their lives. The war had created a physical and emotional wasteland. Reverend Arnold of the Holy Trinity Church in Fareham opened the war memorial to those parishioners lost in the conflict. Two of the names on there were his sons. The younger of the two, Alban Arnold, had died on the Somme, attacking the village of Ovillers with the Royal Fusiliers. In his previous, all too brief existence, he had played for Hampshire, batting attractively during the 1913 and 1914 seasons. *Wisden* reflected that Arnold "would probably have developed into a cricketer of very high class." It is hard to imagine how his father felt as he stood in the rain at the dedication of the memorial. The man standing next to him was Sir Douglas Haig, who had effectively sent his son to his death.

Over two hundred first class cricketers had died "playing the game" between 1914 and 1918. In the depth of all this grief, the fans and players of

81

the post-war era clung to the belief that they had to keep going. This was their legacy. To keep faith with the game they loved, trusting that there was another Golden Age just around the corner.

1914

W. H. Livsey. J. H. Down. A. S. Kennedy. G. Brown. A. Bowell. J. Newman.
J. Stone. H. A. Haig-Smith. A. Jaques. J. G. Greig. C. P. Mead.